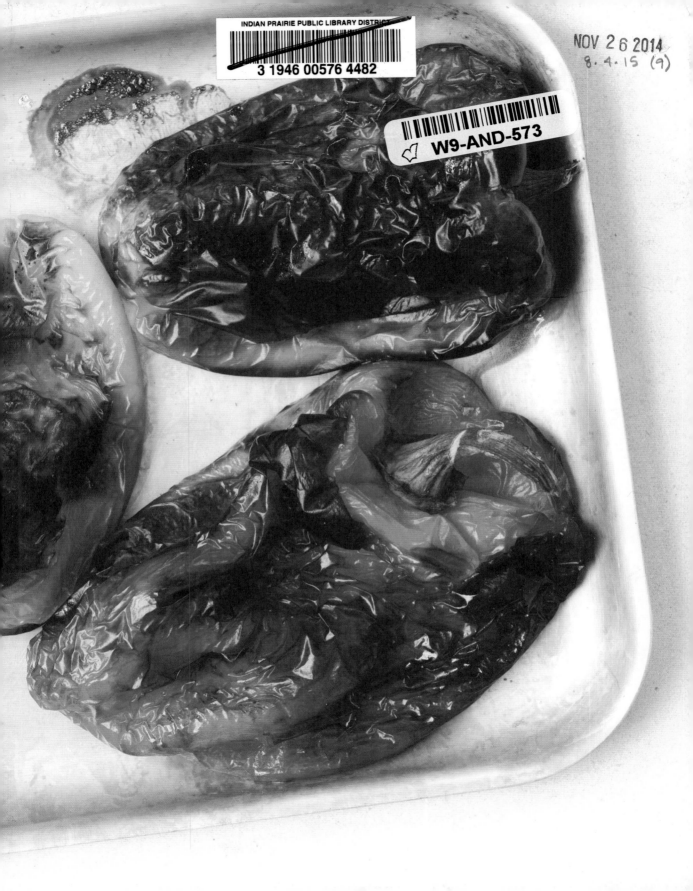

ITALIAN KITCHEN

Anna Del Conte
ITALIAN KITCHEN

PHOTOGRAPHS BY JASON LOWE

STERLING
New York

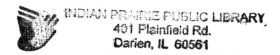

STERLING
New York

An Imprint of Sterling Publishing
387 Park Avenue South
New York, NY 10016

First Sterling edition published in 2014

Originally published in Great Britain by Pavilion Books Ltd.

Photography by Jason Lowe
Original design by Anna Crone at www.siulendesign.com

ISBN 978-1-4549-1078-7

For information about custom editions, special sales, and premium and corporate purchases, please contact
Sterling Special Sales at 800-805-5489 or specialsales@sterlingpublishing.com.

Manufactured in China

2 4 6 8 10 9 7 5 3 1

www.sterlingpublishing.com

Contents

INTRODUCTION

This book is a compendium of four little books I wrote years ago, which were published in 1993 by Pavilion. These were: *Antipasti, Pasta, Risotti,* and *I Dolci*.

The first three books contained my favorite recipes of dishes for which Italian cooking is justly famous.

I decided to write the fourth one, *I Dolci*, for the opposite reason, i.e., because dolci—traditional Italian puddings, cakes, cookies, etc.—are not well known outside of Italy, and some of them are well worth knowing.

Because of its nature, this book contains many vegetarian recipes.

The serving quantity that accompanies each recipe is based on Italian portion sizes, which are typically smaller than American portion sizes.

ANTIPASTI

When I was taken out to dinner as a child, I ate only *l'antipasto*. The trolley would be wheeled next to me and I would be transfixed by the beauty of the food and bewildered by the choice. After a few decades I still feel like that. I want to take all the dishes home, admire them, and eat them slowly and thoughtfully over the next few days. First a taste of prosciutto, as well as *culatello* and *felino*, my favorite salami, which I would eat with bread and nothing else. Next would come a few floppy slices of grilled peppers, a curly tentacle of *calameretti*, and a morsel of each stuffed vegetable. Finally, a spoonful of *nervetti in insalata*—Milanese brawn gleaming with olive oil, crowned with colorful pickled vegetables, and speckled with purple olives and green capers.

Such are the delights of an antipasto offered in a restaurant. When you serve antipasti at home, however, you must be more selective and decide on two or three dishes at most. Otherwise you will be in the kitchen for far too long and begin to hate the idea of an antipasto forever.

An antipasto can provide a good beginning to a meal, and it can even set the style for the meal itself. It is very important that, as an opening to the meal, it should be well presented and pretty to look at. It should also be light and fresh, so as to develop the taste buds for the courses to follow, rather than fill the stomach, and it should harmonize with the rest of the meal.

Nowadays an antipasto is usually a starter, no longer followed by a *primo*—first course—except on special occasions. For instance, if you have decided on a platter of *affettato misto*—mixed cured meats—a generous bowl of tagliatelle dressed with a vigorous sauce would make an ideal follow-on. So also would an earthy risotto or a gutsy spaghetti *alla puttanesca*—with tomatoes, anchovies, and chilies. This is not the traditional Italian way, but it is what suits our smaller stomachs and the advice of health experts.

If, however, you are serving meat, start with a vegetable-based antipasto or a seafood one. A seafood antipasto, indeed, is the ideal precursor to a seafood main course.

The recipes collected here are divided into six sections: Salumi, Bruschetta and Crostini, Salads, Stuffed Vegetables, Seafood and Meat Antipasti, and Other Favorites.

Some of the recipes are for classic antipasto dishes, others are my own or those of my family and friends. All are typically Italian yet very varied—as varied, indeed, as most Italian cooking, because of the great differences between the country's many regions.

Salumi
CURED MEAT PRODUCTS

I know I am an unashamed chauvinist where food is concerned, but I am sure no other country offers such an array of delectable cured meats as Italy does. Salumi are usually made with pork or a mixture of pork and beef. There are also good salumi made with venison and various other meats. The mocetta from Valle d'Aosta is made with wild goat, the bresaola from Valtellina with fillet of beef, the salame d'oca from Friuli and Veneto with goose, and the salami and prosciutti di cinghiale are made with wild boar. This latter is one of the many glories of Tuscany.

The characteristics of the many types of salumi are determined firstly by factors affecting the pig, or other animal, itself. These include its breed, its habitat and food, and the climate of the locality in which it is reared. A prosciutto di Parma is paler and sweeter than, for instance, a prosciutto di montagna—mountain prosciutto. Secondly, salumi differ according to which cuts of meat are used, the proportion of fat to lean, the fineness of the mincing, the flavorings, and the curing.

In what follows I describe some of the salumi that I like to serve as an antipasto. Together they form a dish called *affettato misto*, possibly the most common antipasto served in Italy. This dish of mixed cured meats is pretty to look at in its shades of pink and red, and one of the most appetizing ways to start a meal.

You may be serving the affettato before a dish of pasta. (This is where I should point out that the word antipasto does not mean "before the pasta." It means "before the *pasto*"—meal.) In Italy, however, affettato is often served as a *secondo* for lunch, not before but after the pasta that is de rigueur (only for lunch, though) in any self-respecting Italian family. Still, *primo* or *secondo*, affettato misto is an excellent dish, which, with some good bread or a piece of focaccia, followed by a lovely green salad and some cheese, is a perfect meal in its own right.

A good affettato misto should have a choice of at least five or six different meats. The following is a list of the products you can most easily find outside of Italy. You can mix them to your liking, but one type of prosciutto and two types of salami should always be included. With a prosciutto I put two or three different kinds of salami: one from northern Italy, a Milano perhaps, which is mild and sweet, a peppery salame from the south, and a Roman oval-shaped soppressata. An alternative that I like is a fennel-flavored finocchiona, a salame from Tuscany. A few slices of the best mortadella, speckled with the acid green of fresh pistachio nuts, and of tasty coppa, which is a rolled, cured, and boned shoulder of pork, would be just right for a good assortment.

The prosciutto can be prosciutto di Parma, the sweetest and palest of them all, or prosciutto di San Daniele, made in Friuli, of a darker red and stronger flavor. There is also a prosciutto di Carpegna, which is available in some of the best Italian markets. I like it because it has a good flavor, is usually perfectly salted, and contains the right amount of fat. A good prosciutto should always have some fat.

As for the quantity, I find that about 2 ounces per person is enough. However, it is probably a good idea to buy more, because if you have a few slices left over they come in very handy for a sandwich the next day.

Try to buy your salumi from a delicatessen where it is sliced in front of you, rather than in vacuum packs from a supermarket. It is usually a better product, and you can see with your own eyes if it is really the salumi it purports to be. For instance, prosciutti have a mark of origin, their DOC, stamped on the skin. If you ask for the salumi to be sliced, remember that prosciutto should be sliced fine, but not so fine that you cannot transfer the slice to a dish without breaking it. Salami are better thicker, and the smaller the diameter of the salame, the thicker the cut should be.

Bruschetta e Crostini
GRILLED AND TOASTED BREAD

Bruschetta and crostini are very popular antipasti, and make good "finger food." It is fundamental to the quality of either to use a good chewy type of bread—ciabatta, sourdough, or pain rustique, for example. Here are some classic Italian recipes.

 In Italy, crostini cover a broader range of dishes than bruschetta. Crostini consist of slices of toasted bread moistened with olive oil on which different toppings are spread, while bruschetta is either grilled country bread flavored with olive oil and garlic, or the same grilled bread topped with tomato.

Bruschetta
ROMAN GARLIC BREAD

Bruschetta is a crisp, grilled bread, originally from Rome (*bruscare* means "to burn lightly" in Roman dialect). It is made with coarse country bread, which has a high nutritional value. For centuries bruschetta has been a staple dish of the poor, who ironically used to call it *cappone*—capon—since it was the nearest they could get to this delicacy of the rich. Nowadays bruschetta is served as an appetizer while you wait for your pasta to be ready. Bruschetta is also ideal to eat with seafood soups.

To make bruschetta, cut a good loaf of white bread—ciabatta, Pugliese, pain de campagne, or sourdough—into thick (½–¾ inch) slices. For 6 slices you will need 2–3 smashed garlic cloves, some extra virgin olive oil—preferably a peppery Tuscan oil—and a good deal of freshly ground black pepper.

Score the slices lightly with the point of a small knife in a crisscross fashion. Grill the bread on both sides over charcoal or wood embers (or under the broiler) and then, while still hot, rub it with the garlic. Put the slices in a hot oven for 2 minutes, to make them crisp through, and then place them on a dish. Drizzle about 1 tbsp of oil over each one and sprinkle generously with pepper and a little sea salt.

Bruschetta Tradizionale
CLASSIC BRUSCHETTA

Serves 4

6 tomatoes
sea salt
1 ciabatta loaf
2–3 garlic cloves, cut into
  large pieces
8–9 tbsp extra virgin olive oil
freshly ground black pepper
12 basil leaves, torn into large
  pieces

Bruschetta is now part of the modern culinary repertoire. My only stipulation is that bruschetta with tomatoes must be made with good tomatoes—ripe, sweet, yet full of flavor and with a thin skin, since the tomatoes must not be peeled. Plum tomatoes are particularly suitable, because they do not have many seeds. For the bread, I usually use ciabatta, which is the right size of loaf.

1 Wash and dry the tomatoes. Cut them into small pieces, put on a wooden board, and sprinkle with a little salt, which will bring out the flavor. Leave them for 30–40 minutes.

2 Prepare the bruschetta following the instructions in the last paragraph on page 19, dressing it with the garlic and the oil. Pick up the pieces of tomatoes, leaving the juice behind, and put them on the grilled and dressed bread.

3 Drizzle an additional ½ tsp olive oil over each bruschetta and place a few pieces of basil on top.

Crostini alla Toscana
CHICKEN LIVER CROSTINI

Serves 6–8

8 oz chicken livers
4 tbsp olive oil (for cooking)
½ celery rib, very finely
  chopped
1 shallot, very finely chopped
2 small garlic cloves, chopped
3 tbsp chopped flat-leaf parsley
3½ oz lean ground beef
1 tbsp tomato paste
6 tbsp dry white wine
sea salt and freshly ground
  black pepper
1 tbsp capers, rinsed and
  chopped
2 salted anchovies, boned and
  rinsed, or 4 canned anchovy
  fillets, chopped
2 tbsp unsalted butter

In Tuscany, where this dish comes from, they add calf's melt (the spleen) to the chicken liver. Melt is added only to tone down the flavor of the liver and to give the mixture more volume. Of all offal, melt is the only one that is always used with other types of offal. To give this extra consistency to the mixture, I have substituted ground beef for the melt. It works very well.

You can moisten the bread with Vin Santo mixed with stock, instead of the more common olive oil. Vin Santo is a very strong wine from Chianti, made from grapes that are left to dry for several weeks before they are pressed.

1 Remove the fat, gristle, and any greenish bits from the chicken livers. Wash, dry, and chop as finely as you can.

2 Put the olive oil in a saucepan and, when just hot, add the celery, shallot, garlic, and parsley. Cook for 10 minutes until soft, stirring very frequently.

3 Add the chicken livers and the ground beef and cook gently until the chicken livers have lost their raw color and become crumbly.

4 Mix in the tomato paste and cook for 1 minute. Raise the heat, add the wine, and boil until nearly all the wine has evaporated. Lower the heat and add a little salt and plenty of pepper. Simmer gently for 30 minutes, adding a little hot water if the mixture gets too dry.

5 Mix in the capers and the anchovies. Add the butter and cook gently for 5 minutes, stirring constantly.

6 Spread the mixture on crostini (see page 18) moistened with 1 tbsp olive oil or with a mixture of good chicken stock and Vin Santo.

Puré di Fave
FAVA BEAN PURÉE

Serves 6–8

3 lbs fresh fava beans, or 1 lb
    frozen fava beans
sea salt and freshly ground
    black pepper
3 garlic cloves, peeled
2 oz good-quality crustless
    white bread (about 2 slices)
milk
6 tbsp extra virgin olive oil

For this recipe you can use frozen fava beans which, although they do not have all the sweet mealiness of fresh ones, are picked and frozen at their best. Some recipes suggest using boiled potatoes instead of the bread. Either version is good.

1   Shell the fava beans, if you are using fresh ones. Cook the fresh or frozen beans in a saucepan of simmering water to which you have added 1 tbsp of salt and the garlic. The beans should cook at the lowest simmer. When the beans are tender, drain them and the garlic, reserving a cupful of the water. Allow to cool.

2   Put the bread in a bowl and pour in enough milk just to cover the bread.

3   Now you need to have the patience to slip off the white skin from the beans. It's a rather boring and lengthy job, but it is necessary if you want a really creamy purée without those unpleasant pieces of papery skin. If there are any children around the house, enlist their help; they usually love popping the beans out of their skin.

4   Put the fava beans, garlic, and bread with its milk in a food processor and whiz to a purée, while gradually adding all but about 1 tbsp of the oil through the funnel. Taste and adjust the seasoning, adding a little of the reserved water if too thick.

5   You can spread the purée on crostini (see page 18) moistened with the reserved oil, or serve the purée in a dish surrounded by crostini, and let your guests or family do the work.

Intingolo di Peperoni e Pomodori Secchi

RELISH OF PEPPERS AND SUN-DRIED TOMATOES

Serves 4

2 large red and/or yellow
   peppers
½ sweet onion, very finely
   chopped
2 tbsp extra virgin olive oil
1 garlic clove, very finely
   chopped
½ dried chili, crumbled
2 tsp balsamic vinegar
7 oz sun-dried tomatoes in
   olive oil
1 canned anchovy fillet,
   chopped
1 tbsp capers, rinsed and dried
sea salt and freshly ground
   black pepper

1   Heat the oven to 450° F.

2   Put the peppers on a baking tray and roast in the oven until they are soft, about 30 minutes. Remove from the oven and allow to cool a little.

3   Meanwhile, heat the onion and oil in a small frying pan. Sauté for a few minutes and then add the garlic, chili, and balsamic vinegar, stirring so that the *soffritto* (frying mixture) does not burn. Continue cooking until very soft, stirring frequently.

4   Drain the tomatoes of their preserving oil, cut them into thin strips, and add them to the soffritto. Cook, stirring frequently, for 5 minutes or so.

5   While the tomatoes are cooking, peel the peppers, cut them in half, and discard the core and seeds. Cut them into ½-inch pieces and mix into the soffritto in the pan. Let the peppers *insaporire*—take up the flavor.

6   Add the anchovy fillet to the pan and mash it to a purée. Mix in the capers. Taste and adjust the seasoning. Serve at room temperature with crusty bread or spread on bruschetta.

Fonduta Piemontese
PIEDMONTESE FONDUE

Serves 4

14 oz Italian fontina
1 cup whole milk
4 tbsp unsalted butter
4 large egg yolks
1 white truffle, or 1 tbsp
   truffle paste

Fontina, the best-known cheese from Valle d'Aosta, used to be made at Mont Fontin, from which it takes its name. It is the main ingredient of this classic dish. The other characteristic ingredient is the white truffle of Alba. There are now various brands of truffle paste on the market, made with white truffles and porcini, which works very well in a fonduta. Sliced bread or crostini (see page 18) are served with fonduta for dipping. I also like to use thick slices of grilled polenta.

1   About 6 hours before you want to serve the fonduta, cut the fontina into small dice. Put it in a bowl and add enough milk just to cover the cheese. Set aside. This will help soften the cheese to allow it to melt properly.
2   Put the butter in a heatproof bowl, add the fontina with the milk, and set over a pan of simmering water, taking care that the bottom of the bowl does not touch the water.
3   Cook, stirring constantly, for about 10 minutes until the cheese has melted, then beat in the egg yolks, one at a time. Continue cooking, beating the whole time, until the egg has been absorbed and the sauce reaches the consistency of heavy cream. If you are using truffle paste, mix it in at this point, off the heat.
4   Transfer the fonduta to individual soup dishes and slice the truffle over it, if you are using this food of the gods. Serve immediately.

Insalate
SALADS

A mixed antipasto for a large party, or an antipasto table in a restaurant, usually contains a number of different salads. Grilled peppers, for instance, are a classic antipasto salad, as are tomatoes with mozzarella and basil. The following five recipes include some of my favorites and some classics.

Insalata di Pere e Formaggio
PEAR AND CHEESE SALAD

Serves 4

4 ripe Bartlett or Comice pears
3½ oz Parmigiano-Reggiano
   or good Grana Padano
3½ oz mature pecorino
3 tbsp extra virgin olive oil
2 tbsp lemon juice
sea salt and freshly ground
   black pepper
4 oz arugula

We have a saying in Italy, "Do not let the peasant know how good pears are with cheese"—or he might pick all the pears off your tree. This salad is a sophisticated version of the classic pears with cheese.

1 Peel the pears, cut them into quarters, and remove the cores. Cut each quarter in half and put them in a bowl.
2 Shave the cheese with a vegetable peeler and mix three-quarters of it with the pears.
3 Beat the oil and the lemon juice together and add salt and pepper to taste. Spoon about half this dressing over the pears and leave for 1 hour.
4 Spoon the pears into a deep dish and shower with the remaining cheese. Surround with the arugula and drizzle the rest of the dressing over it. Serve immediately.

Insalata di Broccoli con la Mollica
BROCCOLI AND BREADCRUMB SALAD

Serves 4

1 lb broccoli

6 tbsp extra virgin olive oil

2½ cups fresh breadcrumbs

6 canned anchovy fillets,
   drained, or 3 salted
   anchovies, boned and rinsed

1 or 2 dried chilies, according
   to taste, seeded

2 garlic cloves, peeled

1½ tbsp capers, rinsed and
   dried

12 black olives, pitted and cut
   into strips

sea salt and freshly ground
   black pepper

Brown breadcrumbs are better than white ones for this tasty dish from southern Italy. I make my soft crumbs in a food processor, a very quick job. You can use cauliflower instead of broccoli.

1   Divide the broccoli into small florets. Peel the outer layer from the stalks and cut them into small pieces. Blanch the florets and pieces of stalk in boiling salted water until just tender, about 5 minutes. Drain and dry with paper towels. Transfer to a bowl and add 2 tbsp of the oil. Toss gently using 2 forks, rather than spoons, as they are less likely to break the florets.

2   Heat the rest of the oil in a frying pan and add the breadcrumbs. Cook for 3 minutes, stirring to coat them with the oil.

3   Chop all the other ingredients, except the olives, and add them to the bread mixture. Add the olives and cook for another minute or so, stirring well. Taste and add salt and pepper as necessary.

4   Toss half the breadcrumb mixture into the broccoli and spoon the rest over the top. Serve warm.

Peperoni Arrostiti
GRILLED PEPPERS

Serves 4

4 beautiful red and/or yellow
  peppers
6 canned anchovy fillets,
  drained, or 3 salted
  anchovies, boned and rinsed
3 garlic cloves
2 tbsp chopped flat-leaf parsley
1 small dried chili, seeded
4 tbsp extra virgin olive oil

When peppers are grilled and skinned, their taste is totally different from that of raw or sautéed peppers. To my mind they are much nicer, and they are certainly more digestible. You can prepare a few pounds of peppers when they are in season, and reasonably cheap, and keep them in the fridge in jars, well covered with olive oil, for 2 or 3 months.

1   Using metal tongs, carefully hold the peppers over the flame of a burner, or put them under the broiler. When the side in contact with the heat is charred, turn the pepper until all the surface, including the top and bottom, is charred. As soon as all the skin is charred, remove the pepper from the heat—otherwise the flesh will begin to burn and you will be left with paper-thin peppers.

2   Let the peppers cool and then remove the skin; it will come off very easily as long as the peppers have been well charred. Cut the peppers in half, remove the stem and seeds, then cut the peppers lengthways into strips. Put them on a dish.

3   Pound the anchovies with the garlic, parsley, and chili in a mortar, or chop very finely.

4   Put the oil and the anchovy mixture in a very heavy pan and heat very slowly for about 2 minutes, stirring and pounding the whole time until the mixture is mashed. Spoon the mixture over the peppers and leave to marinate in the refrigerator for at least 4 hours. The longer you leave them—up to a week—the better they get. Serve with plenty of bread.

Pomodori con la Mozzarella e il Basilico

TOMATOES, MOZZARELLA, AND BASIL

Serves 4

12 ripe tomatoes
sea salt and freshly ground
   black pepper
12 oz buffalo mozzarella
6 tbsp extra virgin olive oil
24 fresh basil leaves

This is the simplest and best summer antipasto. However, do not make it unless you have very good tomatoes—tasty and juicy, not woolly and dry. Check out your local farmers' market for the freshest tomatoes, just picked from the vine. Also, use buffalo mozzarella, which has a much deeper flavor than cow's milk mozzarella.

1 Wash and dry the tomatoes and cut them in half. Squeeze out a little of the seeds and juice and sprinkle with salt. Lay the tomato halves on a wooden board, cut side down. Put the board in the fridge for at least 30 minutes.

2 Wipe the inside of the tomatoes with paper towels and place them, cut side up, on a dish.

3 Cut the mozzarella into 24 slices or pieces. Put one piece inside each tomato half. Season with a generous grinding of pepper and drizzle with the olive oil.

4 Wipe the basil leaves with a moistened paper towel. Place a leaf over each piece of mozzarella.

Panzanella
BREAD AND RAW VEGETABLE SALAD

Serves 4

8 thick slices of chewy,
country-style white bread
2–3 tbsp white wine vinegar
12 fresh basil leaves, coarsely
torn
2 garlic cloves, peeled and
finely chopped
½ cucumber, peeled and cut
into ½-inch slices
½ red onion, very thinly sliced
8 oz ripe, meaty tomatoes,
seeded and cut into ½-inch
cubes
sea salt and freshly ground
black pepper
6 tbsp extra virgin olive oil

Panzanella is a traditional rustic salad made in the summer with country bread and seasonal raw vegetables. Make it only when good tomatoes are in season, and with country bread. I recommend a Pugliese loaf, available in good supermarkets or in Italian delicatessens.

1 Cover the bread with cold water to which you have added 1 tbsp of the vinegar. Let soak until just soft, then squeeze out all the liquid and put the bread in a salad bowl. The bread should be damp but not wet. Break it up with a fork.

2 Add the basil, garlic, cucumber, onion, and tomatoes. Season with salt and pepper. Toss thoroughly with the oil, using a fork to turn the mixture over. Chill for 30 minutes or so.

3 Taste and add more vinegar to your liking. It is not possible to specify the amount of vinegar to use, since it depends on its acidity and on personal taste.

Verdure Ripiene
STUFFED VEGETABLES

One of the joys of walking around the old part of Genoa is that you can still see shops selling *farinata* (chickpea tart), *focaccia*, *pissaladeira* (onion pizza), and stuffed vegetables, all in the huge round copper pans in which they have been baked. Fat red tomatoes and shimmering red and yellow peppers fight for space with eggplants of all colors, from purple to ivory, and plump round zucchini, all soft and glistening with oil. The recipes that follow are for my favorite stuffed vegetables. If you choose two or three of them to serve together, you are sure to give your family and friends one of the most appetizing and satisfying antipasti ever.

   The tomatoes, peppers, and zucchini, for instance, go together very well, while the eggplants are perfect also by themselves. All these stuffed vegetables are best served warm or at room temperature, but not hot or chilled. They are even more delicious if made a day in advance.

Funghi Ripieni alla Genovese
STUFFED MUSHROOM CAPS

Serves 4

¾ oz dried porcini
1 lb large-cap mushrooms
1 cup fresh white breadcrumbs
1 salted anchovy, boned and
  rinsed, or 2 canned anchovy
  fillets, drained
1 or 2 garlic cloves, according
  to taste, peeled
handful of fresh marjoram
pinch of grated nutmeg
sea salt and freshly ground
  black pepper
4 tbsp extra virgin olive oil
2 tbsp chopped flat-leaf parsley

If you can find them, use fresh porcini. Otherwise you can use cultivated large mushrooms, plus a little dried porcini for better flavor, as in this recipe.

1 Soak the dried porcini in a cupful of very hot water for 30 minutes. If necessary, rinse under cold water to remove any trace of grit. Dry thoroughly with paper towels.

2 Gently wipe the large-cap mushrooms with a damp cloth and detach the stalks.

3 Chop together the dried porcini, mushroom stalks, breadcrumbs, anchovies, garlic, and marjoram. You can use a food processor, but do not reduce to pulp. Transfer to a bowl and add the nutmeg, salt, and pepper to taste.

4 Heat the oven to 425°F.

5 Heat 2 tbsp of the oil in a frying pan and add the mushroom and breadcrumb mixture. Sauté for 5 minutes, stirring frequently.

6 Lay the mushroom caps on an oiled baking sheet, hollow side up. Sprinkle them with salt and then fill them with the crumb mixture. Sprinkle a pinch or two of parsley on top of each cap and then drizzle with the remaining oil. Bake for 10–15 minutes until the caps are soft. Serve at room temperature.

Melanzane Ripiene

EGGPLANT STUFFED WITH SAUSAGE, PINE NUTS, AND CURRANTS

Serves 4

2 eggplants, about 1 lb each
sea salt and freshly ground
    black pepper
4 tbsp extra virgin olive oil
1 large garlic clove, finely
    chopped
½ small onion or 1 shallot,
    very finely chopped
½ celery rib, very finely
    chopped
8 oz spicy luganega or other
    spicy, coarse-grained, pure
    pork Italian sausage,
    skinned and crumbled
⅔ cup soft white breadcrumbs
3 tbsp pine nuts
2 tbsp capers, rinsed and dried
1 large egg
1 tbsp dried oregano
3 tbsp freshly grated pecorino
    or Parmesan
3 tbsp dried currants
1 large ripe tomato

1   Wash and dry the eggplant. Cut in half lengthways and scoop out all the flesh with the help of a small sharp knife and then with a small teaspoon, leaving just enough flesh to cover the skin. Be careful not to pierce the skin.

2   Chop the flesh of the eggplant coarsely and place in a colander. Sprinkle with salt, mix well, and leave to drain for about 1 hour.

3   Heat the oven to 375°F.

4   Put 3 tbsp of the oil and the garlic, onion, and celery in a frying pan and sauté over a low heat until soft, stirring frequently. Add the sausage and cook for 20 minutes, stirring frequently.

5   Meanwhile, squeeze the liquid from the chopped eggplant flesh and dry thoroughly with paper towels. Add the eggplant flesh to the pan and fry gently for a few minutes, stirring frequently. Taste and adjust the seasoning.

6   Add the breadcrumbs to the mixture in the frying pan. After 2–3 minutes, mix in the pine nuts. Cook for another 30 seconds, then transfer to a bowl.

7   Add the capers, egg, oregano, cheese, currants, and pepper to taste to the mixture and blend very thoroughly. Taste and add salt if necessary.

8   Pat dry the inside of the eggplant shells. Oil a baking dish large enough to hold the eggplant shells in a single layer. Place the eggplant shells, one next to the other, in the dish and fill them with the sausage mixture.

9   Core and deseed the tomato, then cut it into strips and place 2 or 3 strips on top of each eggplant half. Drizzle with the rest of the oil. Add ½ cup of water to the bottom of the dish. Cover the dish tightly with foil and bake for 20 minutes. Remove the foil and bake for another 20 minutes. This dish is best eaten warm, an hour or so after it comes out of the oven.

Pomodori Ammollicati

TOMATOES STUFFED WITH BREADCRUMBS AND PARSLEY

Serves 3 or 4

6 large round tomatoes, ripe
    but firm
sea salt and freshly ground
    black pepper
2 tbsp chopped flat-leaf
    parsley
2 garlic cloves, finely chopped
1 tbsp capers, rinsed and
    chopped
½ small dried chili, chopped
4 tbsp dried white breadcrumbs
½ tbsp dried oregano
5 tbsp extra virgin olive oil

1   Cut the tomatoes in half. Remove the seeds and sprinkle with salt. Lay them cut side down on a wooden board to drain for about 30 minutes. Wipe the inside of each half with paper towels.

2   Heat the oven to 350°F.

3   Put the parsley, garlic, capers, chili, breadcrumbs, and oregano in a bowl. Mix well and then add 4 tbsp of the oil. Season with a little salt and some pepper. Mix well to a paste.

4   Oil the bottom of a shallow baking dish or roasting pan. Place the tomatoes in the dish, cut side up.

5   Spoon a little of the breadcrumb mixture into each tomato half and drizzle the rest of the oil over the top. Bake for about 30 minutes, until the tomatoes are soft but still whole. Serve at room temperature.

Peperoni Ammollicati
PEPPERS STUFFED WITH BREADCRUMBS AND PARSLEY

Serves 4

1½ lbs red and yellow peppers
5 tbsp extra virgin olive oil
sea salt and freshly ground
 black pepper
3 tbsp chopped flat-leaf
 parsley
2 garlic cloves, finely chopped
1 tbsp capers, rinsed and
 chopped
½ small dried chili, chopped
2 salted anchovies, boned,
 rinsed, and chopped
4 tbsp dried white breadcrumbs

The stuffing for peppers is basically the same as that for tomatoes. I prefer, however, to omit the oregano and to add salted anchovies. Use red and yellow peppers, but not green because they are not sweet enough.

1 Heat the oven to 350°F.
2 Cut the peppers into quarters and remove the cores, ribs, and seeds. Heat 4 tbsp of the oil in a large frying pan until very hot and then add the peppers, skin side down. Sprinkle with salt and pepper and cook for about 10 minutes, shaking the pan occasionally.
3 Mix together the remaining ingredients in a bowl.
4 When the peppers are just soft, place them in an oiled baking dish, cut side up. Pour the juices from the pan into the breadcrumb mixture and mix well. Taste to check the seasoning.
5 Place a small mound of stuffing into each piece of pepper, drizzle with the remaining oil, and bake for 15 minutes.

Zucchine al Forno
BAKED ZUCCHINI WITH MINT AND GARLIC STUFFING

Serves 4

1 lb medium zucchini
sea salt and freshly ground
  black pepper
2 tbsp chopped flat-leaf parsley
4 tbsp chopped fresh mint
2 garlic cloves, chopped
4 tbsp dried breadcrumbs
6 tbsp extra virgin olive oil

1 Cut the zucchini in half lengthways. Make some diagonal incisions on the cut side. Sprinkle the cut side lightly with salt and place the zucchini halves on a wooden board, cut side down. This will allow some of the liquid to drain away.

2 Heat the oven to 350°F.

3 Put the chopped herbs in a bowl and add the garlic and breadcrumbs. Add half the oil gradually, while beating with a fork. Season with a good grinding of pepper and with very little salt.

4 Oil a shallow baking dish or a lasagne dish large enough to hold all the zucchini halves in a single layer.

5 Wipe the zucchini halves with paper towels and lay them in the dish, cut side up. Spoon a little of the herb mixture over each half. Drizzle 1 tbsp of the oil over the halves and cover the dish with foil. Bake for 30 minutes. Remove the foil and continue baking until the zucchini is tender and the top is crisp, about 10 minutes longer.

6 Drizzle with the remaining oil while the zucchini is still hot. Serve warm or at room temperature.

Antipasti di Pesce e Carne
SEAFOOD AND MEAT ANTIPASTI

The following recipes are for dishes whose main ingredient, whether seafood or meat, is usually served as a main course. In these recipes the seafood and meat are prepared in a light and lively way that is extremely appetizing and therefore particularly suited to an antipasto.

Cozze Ripiene
STUFFED MUSSELS

Serves 4

2 lbs mussels
2 organic lemons, cut into
   quarters
6 garlic cloves, peeled
½ cup extra virgin olive oil
5 tbsp chopped flat-leaf parsley
5 tbsp dried breadcrumbs
sea salt and freshly ground
   black pepper

This is the basic recipe for *cozze ripiene*, to which other ingredients such as grated pecorino, tomato sauce, capers, and so on can be added.

1   Mussels are much cleaner these days, because they are usually farmed. However, they still need a good cleaning. Put them in a sink full of cold water and scrub them with a stiff brush. Scrape off any barnacles and beards. Discard any mussel that stays open after tapping it against a hard surface: it is dead. Rinse the mussels in several changes of water until the water is clean and no sand is left at the bottom of the sink.

2   Put the lemon quarters and 5 cloves of garlic in a large frying pan. Add the mussels, cover, and cook over high heat until the mussels are open. Shake the pan occasionally. (Discard any that remain closed. They might be full of sand.)

3   Heat the oven to 425°F.

4   Remove the top of each mussel shell. Loosen the mussels in the bottom shell and place them on a baking sheet.

5   Filter the mussel liquid left in the pan through a sieve lined with cheesecloth into a bowl. Mix in the oil, parsley, and breadcrumbs, and salt and pepper to taste. Finely chop the remaining garlic and add to the mixture.

6   Place a little of the parsley and breadcrumb mixture over each mussel and bake for about 7 minutes, until golden brown.

Insalata Calda di Mare
WARM SEAFOOD SALAD

In this popular antipasto dish you can vary the fish you use according to your taste and the availability of the fish in the market. Remember to have a good selection of textures, but do not use any kind of bluefish as its taste would be too strong. I like to serve this seafood salad warm.

Serves 6

1 lb mussels
1 dried chili, left whole
1 lb squid
4 tbsp wine vinegar
1 onion, cut in half
2 bay leaves
sea salt and freshly ground
    black pepper
12 oz monkfish
8 oz shelled scallops
12 large raw prawns in shell,
    about 8 oz
1 garlic clove, finely chopped
3 tbsp chopped flat-leaf parsley
3 tbsp lemon juice
 cup extra virgin olive oil
black olives, to garnish

1 Put the mussels in a sink full of cold water and scrub them with a stiff brush, scraping off any barnacles and beards with a small knife. Discard any open mussel that fails to close after being tapped hard on a hard surface. Rinse the mussels in several changes of water until the water is clean and no sand is left at the bottom of the sink.

2 Put the mussels in a large saucepan, cover, and cook over high heat until they are open, shaking the pan every now and then. Discard any mussels that remain closed. Shell the mussels and put the meat in a bowl; discard the shells. Filter the liquid through a fine sieve lined with cheesecloth, then pour the clear liquid over the mussels. Pour it very gently so that any sand is left on the bottom of the pan. Add the chili for flavoring.

3 Ask your fishmonger to clean and skin the squid. If he is not prepared to do it, proceed as follows. Hold the sac in one hand and pull off the tentacles with the other hand. The contents of the sac will come out,

too. Cut the tentacles above the eyes. Squeeze out the thin bony beak in the center of the tentacles. Peel off the skin from the sac and the flap. Remove the translucent backbone from inside the sac and rinse the sac and tentacles under cold water. Cut the sac into strips and the tentacles into bite-size pieces.

4 Put about 6 cups of cold water in a saucepan, add 2 tbsp of the vinegar, the onion, 1 bay leaf, and some salt, and bring to a boil. Add the squid and cook over a steady simmer for 5–15 minutes, depending on their size. Squid are cooked when they become white and lose their translucency and you can pierce them with a fork. Remove the squid from the water with a slotted spoon, drain well, and add to the mussels in the bowl.

5 Cut the monkfish into large chunks and add to the boiling water in which the squid have cooked. Simmer gently for about 2 minutes. Remove from the heat, leaving the fish in the liquid.

6 While the monkfish is cooking, put another saucepan on the heat with about 2½ cups of hot water, the remaining bay leaf, the rest of the vinegar, and some salt. When the water is boiling, add the scallops. Simmer for 2 minutes after the water has returned to a boil and then remove with a slotted spoon. If the scallops are large, cut them into quarters. Add to the bowl containing the mussels and squid.

7 Put the prawns into the boiling water in which the scallops have cooked. Simmer for 1 minute after the water has come back to a boil. Drain and set aside to cool.

8 Drain the monkfish. Remove any bone and skin and cut into bite-size pieces. Add the fish to the bowl with the other seafood.

9 Peel the prawns and, if necessary, devein them. Cut them into rounds and add to the bowl.

10 Prepare the sauce: Mix the garlic, parsley, and lemon juice together in a small bowl. Add a generous grinding of black pepper and some salt. Beat in the oil slowly. Taste and adjust the seasonings.

11 Before serving, put the bowl containing the seafood over a saucepan of simmering water. Cover the bowl and heat until the fish is warm, not hot. Stir it once or twice using a fork, not a spoon, which could break the pieces of fish.

12 Fish the chili out of the bowl and discard it. Spoon the sauce over the seafood and toss gently but thoroughly. Pile the seafood salad in a deep dish and scatter the olives over it.

Magroni di Anatra all'Aceto Balsamico

DUCK BREASTS WITH BALSAMIC VINEGAR

Serves 6

2 duck breasts, about
   12 oz each
sea salt and freshly ground
   black pepper
2–3 tbsp balsamic vinegar,
   according to taste and acidity
8 oz mâche (also known as
   lamb's lettuce)
3 tbsp extra virgin olive oil

Balsamic vinegar is a superb condiment for duck. The sauce it produces when mixed with the cooking juices is rich in flavor and yet tangy enough to cut through the richness of the meat. I like to serve this duck with a light salad of mâche, as its lemony flavor and fresh crispness tone down the fattiness of the duck. If you cannot find mâche, use curly endive cut into thin strips.

1   Score the skin of the duck breasts with the point of a small, sharp knife. Rub with salt and pepper.
2   Heat a frying pan. Place the breasts in the pan, skin side down, and cook over moderate heat for 7–9 minutes, depending on their thickness. The fat will run out. Pour out nearly all the fat. Save it, covered and refrigerated, for sautéing potatoes in the future.
3   Spoon 1 tbsp of balsamic vinegar over the breasts and turn them over. Cook for 2 minutes on the underside. Lift out the breasts and place on a board. Carve across into scant ¼-inch-thick slices. Place the slices on a warm dish. Cover with foil and let sit for 10 minutes, for the meat to relax.
4   Add the remaining balsamic vinegar and about 4 tbsp hot water to the frying pan and stir well to deglaze the juices. Taste to see if you need a little more vinegar and/or water.
5   Toss the mâche with the oil and season with a little salt and a generous grinding of pepper. Make a bed of mâche on each plate.
6   Place the duck slices on the mâche and drizzle the juices from the pan over the meat and mâche. Do not wait too long to serve the dish after you have poured the juices or the lettuce will wilt too much.

Sarde a Beccaficu
STUFFED SARDINES

Serves 6

2 lbs fresh sardines
4 tbsp dried currants
5 tbsp olive oil
1½ cups dried white
   breadcrumbs
4 tbsp pine nuts
1 garlic clove, finely chopped
2 tbsp chopped flat-leaf parsley
2 tbsp grated aged pecorino
sea salt and freshly ground
   black pepper
12 bay leaves
juice of 1 organic orange
juice of ½ organic lemon
1 tsp sugar

The combination of sardines and orange is found only in Sicily, and this dish produces the best of this unusual yet delicious mixture of flavors. An antipasto that is very popular in Palermo and Messina, it is a peasant dish whose name derives from its appearance. The boned sardines are rolled up around a spoonful of stuffing and set in a dish with their tails in the air, making them look like fat little *beccafichi*—warblers—pecking at the dish.

1   Few fishmongers are willing to prepare the sardines for you, so this is what you should do. Cut off the heads and the fins (but not the tail), slit the belly, and clean out the insides. Lay the sardines on a board, open side down, and press the backbone down gently. Cut the backbone at the tail end and remove it. Wash and dry the fish.

2   Put the currants in a bowl and cover with boiling water. Let sit for 5–10 minutes to plump up. Drain and dry them thoroughly with paper towels.

3   Heat 3 tbsp of the oil in a frying pan and fry the breadcrumbs until nicely browned. Mix in the pine nuts, garlic, parsley, and currants. Sauté gently for a few minutes and then remove the pan from the heat. Add the cheese and pepper to taste. Taste and add salt if necessary.

4   Heat the oven to 350°F.

5   Sprinkle the sardines on both sides with a little salt and pepper and place them skin side down. Spread a generous teaspoonful of stuffing over each fish and roll up towards the tail. Place the sardines in an oiled baking dish with the tails sticking up in the air.

6   Stick the bay leaves here and there among the little bundles. Drizzle the orange and lemon juices and the rest of the oil all over, then sprinkle with the sugar.

7   Place the dish in the oven and bake for 15–20 minutes, depending on the size of the fish. Serve at room temperature.

Sfogi in Saor
SOLE FILLETS IN A SWEET-AND-SOUR SAUCE

Serves 6–8

flour for coating the fish
sea salt
oil for deep frying
1½ lbs sole fillets
⅓ cup raisins
2 tbsp olive oil
8 oz sweet onions, thinly
　　sliced
2 tsp sugar
½ cup good wine vinegar
4 bay leaves
½ cup pine nuts
2–3 pinches of ground
　　cinnamon
2 cloves
12 black peppercorns,
　　lightly smashed

The taste of this sauce, in which the sole is marinated for 2 days, is strongly reminiscent of Middle Eastern cooking. This is understandable as this dish originated in Venice, a city that in the past had important trade links with the Orient.

Sfogi in saor (Venetian dialect for *sogliole in sapore*, meaning "sole in a sauce") is one of the dishes traditionally eaten in Venice during the Feast of the Redeemer, which falls on the third Sunday in July, when the lagoon is lit by thousands of fireworks and carpeted with boats of every size.

1　Spread some flour on a board and season with salt.
2　Heat oil for deep frying in a wok or a frying pan. Meanwhile, coat the fish lightly in the flour.
3　When the oil is very hot but not smoking (test by frying a small piece of bread; it should brown in 50 seconds), slide in the sole fillets, a few at a time. Fry gently for about 3 minutes on each side until a golden crust has formed. Using a slotted spatula, transfer the fish to a plate lined with paper towels to drain.
4　Soak the raisins in a little warm water to plump them.
5　Heat the olive oil and onions in a small frying pan. Add a pinch of salt and the sugar. Cook the onions gently, stirring frequently, until golden. Turn up the heat and pour in the wine vinegar. Boil briskly until the liquid is reduced by half.
6　Lay the fish neatly in a shallow dish. Pour the onion sauce over the fish and put the bay leaves on top. Drain the raisins and scatter them on top of the dish together with the pine nuts, spices, and peppercorns. Cover the dish with plastic wrap and let marinate for 24 hours. If you want to keep the dish for 2 days or more, refrigerate it. Take the dish out of the fridge at least 2 or 3 hours before you want to serve it, so that it has time to reach room temperature.

Il Mio Carpaccio
MY CARPACCIO

Serves 4

12 oz fillet of beef
1 egg yolk
¾ cup extra virgin olive oil
3 tbsp lemon juice
1 tsp Dijon mustard
a few drops of Tabasco sauce
sea salt and freshly ground
    black pepper

Created by Giuseppe Cipriani at Harry's Bar for one of his clients who was on a strict diet, carpaccio has now become the byword for any fish or meat served raw and dressed with some sort of olive oil–based sauce. Each cook varies the sauce according to his or her preference, so you can experiment with your carpaccio. This is my version.

I use an electric carving knife to slice the beef very thinly, but if you do not have one, carve the meat, then put the slices between 2 sheets of plastic wrap and pound with a meat pounder or rolling pin to make them thinner.

1 Put the beef in the freezer for about 3 hours to harden it; this makes it easier to slice thinly.
2 Put the egg yolk in a food processor with 2 tbsp of the oil, the lemon juice, mustard, Tabasco, and some salt and pepper and process for 30 seconds.
3 Add the rest of the oil slowly through the processor funnel. The sauce will become like a thin mayonnaise. Taste and adjust the seasoning.
4 Remove the beef from the freezer and place on a board. Using an electric carving knife, or a *very* sharp knife, slice it very thinly. Allow the meat to come back to room temperature—about 1 hour.
5 Arrange the meat neatly on individual plates and drizzle the sauce over it before serving. Season lightly with salt and pepper.

OTHER FAVORITES

These are recipes I wanted to include, but which did not fit into any of the other categories.

Radicchio Rosso e Cicoria Belga Alla Trevisana
GRILLED RADICCHIO AND ENDIVE

Serves 6

1 lb red radicchio
½ lb endive
6 tbsp extra virgin olive oil
sea salt and freshly ground
  black pepper

The radicchio rosso used in Veneto for this dish is the long radicchio of Treviso, which can sometimes be found in specialty green markets during the autumn. It has the characteristic bitterness of radicchio, with a delicate yet more pronounced flavor than the round rosa di Chioggia, which is the kind of radicchio available everywhere year-round. The rosa di Chioggia is a modern type of radicchio that is grown in greenhouses. It is tougher and blander, with a similarity to white cabbage. However, the use of heat in this recipe brings out its flavor.

1 Heat the grill (or broiler).
2 Wash the radicchio and endive carefully. Dry thoroughly. Cut the radicchio into quarters and the endive in half, both lengthwise.
3 Place the radicchio and endive in the grill pan (or in a broiler pan). Drizzle the oil over the vegetables and season with salt and a generous amount of pepper.
4 Cook on the grill (or under the broiler) for 10 minutes, taking care to turn the heat down if the vegetables start to burn. Turn the pieces over halfway through the cooking. The vegetables are ready when the thick core can be pierced easily with a sharp knife.
5 Transfer the grilled vegetables to a dish and spoon over the juice from the pan. Serve hot or at room temperature.

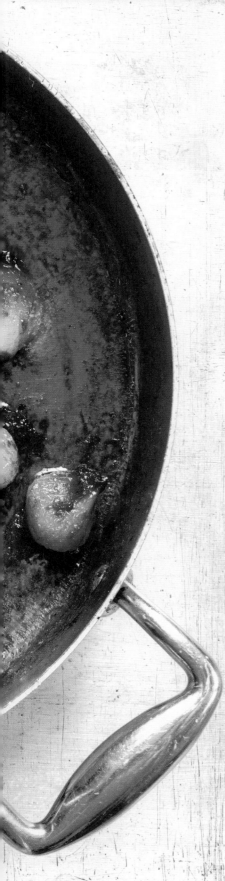

Cipolline Brasate
BRAISED BABY ONIONS

These onions, served at room temperature, often form part of a spectacular Piedmontese antipasto. They can also accompany cold meat or, served hot, boiled or braised meat dishes. The onions used in Italy are white, squat cipolline, very sweet in taste. If you can't find cipolline, use small, young pickling onions instead.

Serves 4

1½ lbs small onions
4 tbsp olive oil
1 tbsp butter
2 tsp tomato paste dissolved in ⅔ cup hot water
2 tbsp sugar
2 tbsp red wine vinegar
sea salt and freshly ground black pepper

1 Put the onions in a pan of boiling water. Bring back to a boil and blanch for 1 minute. Drain and remove the outside skin, taking care to remove only the dangling roots and not the base of the root—otherwise the onions will fall apart while cooking.
2 Choose a large sauté pan and add the onions, olive oil, and butter. Sauté the onions until golden, shaking the pan often.
3 Add the diluted tomato paste, sugar, vinegar, and salt and pepper to taste. Cook, uncovered, for about 1 hour, adding a little more water if necessary. The onions are ready when they are a rich brown color and can easily be pierced by a fork. Serve hot or at room temperature, but not chilled.

Frittelle di Mozzarella
MOZZARELLA AND PARMESAN FRITTERS

Serves 4

8 oz fresh mozzarella
1 large egg
¾ cup freshly grated Parmesan
2 tbsp flour
12 fresh basil leaves
1 small garlic clove, finely
  chopped
sea salt and freshly ground
  black pepper
oil for deep frying

1   Place the fresh mozzarella in a sieve placed over a bowl and let sit for 3–4 hours to drain the liquid. Grate the mozzarella through the largest holes of a cheese grater and put it in a bowl.

2   Beat the egg lightly and add to the bowl with the Parmesan and flour.

3   Wipe the basil leaves with damp paper towels and snip them with scissors. Mix into the mozzarella mixture with the garlic, a generous grinding of pepper, and a little salt. (Add salt with caution because the Parmesan is already salty.) Mix thoroughly.

4   With damp hands, shape the mixture into small balls, each the size of a walnut. If the mixture is too loose, add a little more flour. Put the balls on a wooden board and chill for at least 30 minutes.

5   Heat oil in a wok or a small, deep saucepan. When the oil is very hot but not yet smoking (the right temperature is 350°F, i.e. when a small piece of bread turns golden in 50 seconds) slide in the cheese balls in batches. Do not crowd the pan or they will not fry properly. Turn them over and when they are a deep golden color all over, fish them out with a slotted spoon and transfer to paper towels to drain. Serve hot.

Carote in Agrodolce
CARROTS IN A WINE AND HERB SAUCE

Serves 6

2 lbs carrots
6 tbsp olive oil
1 cup dry white wine
½ cup white wine vinegar
2 sprigs of fresh flat-leaf
   parsley
2 sprigs of fresh thyme
4 fresh sage leaves
2 bay leaves
4 sprigs of fresh mint
2 garlic cloves, cut in half
sea salt and freshly ground
   black pepper
2 tbsp sugar

Carrots are underrated vegetables. This sweet-and-sour sauce transforms them into an ideal autumn or winter antipasto.

1 Cut the carrots into thick matchsticks and put them in a sauté pan.
2 Add all the other ingredients plus 1 cup of water. Bring to a boil and cook, uncovered, for 30 minutes. The carrots will still be quite crunchy.
3 Lift the carrots out of the pan with a slotted spoon and transfer to a bowl. Set aside.
4 Boil the liquid that remains in the pan rapidly to reduce until it is very tasty and has a beautiful deep golden color. Most of the water will have evaporated and you will be left with a delicious, hot, herby vinaigrette. Taste and adjust the seasoning.
5 Pour the reduced liquid over the carrots and let marinate at room temperature for 48 hours.
6 Remove the herbs and garlic before serving.

Caponata
EGGPLANT, ONION, AND CELERY STEW

Serves 4

1½ lbs eggplant
the inner ribs of 1 celery head,
   coarse threads removed
vegetable oil for frying
sea salt and freshly ground
   black pepper
½ cup olive oil
1 onion, very finely sliced
8 oz Italian canned plum
   tomatoes, chopped
1 tbsp sugar
⅓ cup white wine vinegar
1 tbsp grated bittersweet
   chocolate (70% cocoa solids)
¼ cup capers
2 oz large green olives, pitted
   and quartered
2 hard-boiled eggs

Thanks to Sicilian creativity, the humble eggplant here forms the basis of one of the grandest vegetable dishes. Caponata appears in many versions throughout the island. It can be garnished with tiny boiled octopus, a small lobster, prawns, or *bottarga*—the air-dried roe of the gray mullet, a speciality of Sardinia. I garnish this one with hard-boiled eggs, making it a perfect vegetarian dish.

The secret of a good caponata is cooking the three vegetables—eggplant, celery, and onion—separately and only then combining them with the other ingredients.

1 Cut the eggplant and celery into equal-size pieces. Heat an inch of vegetable oil in a frying pan. When the oil is hot (it is ready when it sizzles around a cube of eggplant), add a layer of eggplant and fry until golden brown on all sides. Drain on paper towels. Repeat until all of the eggplant is cooked. Season each batch lightly with salt.

2 Fry the celery in the same oil until golden and crisp. Drain on paper towels.

3 Pour the olive oil into a clean frying pan and add the onion. Sauté gently for about 10 minutes until soft. Add the tomatoes and cook, stirring frequently, over a moderate heat for about 15 minutes. Season with salt and pepper.

4 While the sauce is cooking, heat the sugar and vinegar in a small saucepan. Add the chocolate, capers, and olives and cook gently until the chocolate has melted. Add to the tomato sauce and cook for 5 minutes.

5 Mix the eggplant and celery into the tomato sauce. Stir and cook for 20 minutes so that the flavors of the ingredients can blend together. Pour the caponata into a serving dish and allow to cool.

6 Pass the hard-boiled eggs through the smallest holes of a food mill, or push through a metal sieve. Before serving, cover the caponata with the sieved eggs.

Bagna Caôda
HOT GARLICKY DIP FOR RAW VEGETABLES

Serves 4–6

assortment of raw vegetables
such as cardoons, celery,
cauliflower, zucchini, carrots,
radishes, and bell peppers
5 tbsp unsalted butter
5 garlic cloves, very finely
sliced or chopped
2 oz salted anchovies, boned,
rinsed, and chopped, or
canned anchovy fillets,
chopped
⅔ cup extra virgin olive oil
sea salt

Bagna caôda is a peasant dish from Piedmont, where it is made in earthenware pots kept hot on glowing embers. A small, deep earthenware pot is by far the best receptacle in which to make it. You will also need a warming tray or candle burner in the middle of the table to keep the bagna caôda hot, though it must not cook. The vegetables are dipped, raw, into the sauce, although some cooks prefer to blanch the cardoons and celery. Plenty of crusty bread and full-bodied red wine, such as a dolcetto, Barolo, or nebbiolo, are the other essentials. The olive oil used should be a mild extra virgin one from Liguria, not a peppery oil from Tuscany.

1 First prepare the vegetables. Cardoons are the traditional vegetable for bagna caôda, but they are not easy to find. If you find some, they will usually have already had their outer leaves and tough stalks removed. You will have to remove the strings, as you do with celery sticks. Cut the stalks and the heart into suitable pieces. Rub any cut part with lemon to prevent discoloring. Prepare all the other vegetables as you would for a normal dip, i.e. washing, scraping, stringing, according to the vegetable, and then cutting into sticks or other bite-size pieces. Choose the best specimens and discard any bruised parts.

2 Melt the butter in a small, deep earthenware pot or a very heavy-bottomed saucepan over the lowest heat. As soon as the butter has melted and begun to foam, add the garlic and cook for a minute or so. The garlic should not color. Add the anchovies to the pot and pour in the oil very gradually, stirring the whole time. Cook for about 10 minutes, always on the lowest possible heat and stirring constantly. The sauce should never come close to boiling. The dip is ready when the anchovies have dissolved into the oil mixture. Taste and add salt if necessary. Pepper is not added to traditional bagna caôda.

3 Bring the pot to the table together with the prepared vegetables, and place it over a low flame or on a warming tray.

Uova Soda alla Pugliese con i Pomodori Secchi

HARD-BOILED EGGS WITH PARSLEY, BREADCRUMB TOPPING, AND SUN-DRIED TOMATOES

Serves 4

8 oz sun-dried tomatoes in
   olive oil
6 large eggs
6 tbsp extra virgin olive oil
6 tbsp dried white breadcrumbs
2 tbsp good red wine vinegar
   (not balsamic vinegar)
3 garlic cloves, chopped
6 tbsp chopped flat-leaf
   parsley
2–3 dried chilies, according to
   taste, chopped
sea salt and freshly ground
   black pepper

These eggs are served at room temperature. I like to surround them with charred and peeled yellow and red peppers (page 35) or, as here, with sun-dried tomatoes generously dressed with extra virgin olive oil and seasoned with garlic, salt, and pepper. I also like to scatter black olives around the dish.

1   Drain the tomatoes of their preserving oil and set aside while you prepare the eggs.

2   Hard-boil the eggs: lower them into a pan of simmering water and cook for 8 minutes, no longer, so that the yolks will be just set. Put the saucepan under cold running water for 1 minute. Crack the shells and peel them off. Let the eggs cool in the cold water while you make the topping.

3   Heat 3 tbsp of the oil in a small frying pan. Add the breadcrumbs and sauté for a couple of minutes, stirring constantly, until the crumbs are golden. Add 1 tbsp of the remaining oil to the pan with the vinegar and all the other ingredients. Sauté gently for another couple of minutes. Taste and adjust the seasoning.

4   Drain and dry the eggs. Cut them in half lengthwise. To prevent the egg halves from sliding on the dish, slice off a tiny bit of the white on the round side to give a flat base. Arrange the eggs on a serving dish and drizzle with the remaining oil. Season lightly with salt and pepper and spoon about 2 tsp of the topping over each egg half. To serve, arrange the drained tomatoes around the eggs.

"I like all simple things, boiled eggs, oysters
and caviar, *truite au bleu*, grilled salmon,
roast lamb (the saddle by preference),
cold grouse, treacle tart, and rice pudding.
But of all simple things the only one I can eat
day in and day out, not only without disgust
but with the eagerness of an appetite
unimpaired by excess, is macaroni."

From a short story, "The Hairless Mexican" by
W. SOMERSET MAUGHAM

PASTA

Pasta is the simplest food, even simpler than bread, consisting only of semolina and water for dried pasta and flour and eggs for homemade pasta. It is also the food that can change its character and appearance more than any other, like some great character actor assuming countless different roles. Think of the golden lightness of a delicate dish of tagliatelle with butter and compare it to the intriguing flavor of a dish of spaghetti with green pesto, or the rich earthiness of a baked lasagne. All are equally good in their different ways, and pasta is the main ingredient of them all.

TYPES OF PASTA

We Italians never look down on dried pasta. We consider it ideal for many sauces and would never regard it as merely a substitute for homemade pasta. Good factory-produced dried pasta is made from durum wheat ground into semolina and mixed with water into a dough. The dough is forced through perforated metal discs to form the desired shape, and then dried. Dried pasta should be buff-yellow, translucent, and slightly shiny. The most common kinds are long pasta of various widths and lengths such as spaghetti; shapes such as fusilli, penne, and conchiglie; lasagne; and small pastas for soups. The "fresh pasta" sold in delicatessens or supermarkets is made with durum wheat semolina, flour, eggs, and water. Though it is convenient, it certainly is not as good as homemade pasta, and it compares badly with dried pasta of a good Italian brand.

Homemade pasta has a lightness and delicacy that store-bought "fresh pasta" cannot match. So, when you want to make a recipe that calls for fresh pasta, do try to make it yourself, whether by hand or with the help of a machine. Remember, though, that it is not easy to make pasta by hand without practice, time, and a long, thin pasta rolling pin.

Luckily there are good machines to speed up the task. Some electric machines make good pasta, but they are expensive, noisy, and difficult to clean. The hand-cranked machines are cheap and easily obtained.

COOKING PASTA

It is easy to cook pasta, but it can be spoiled by carelessness. Pasta needs to be cooked in a large saucepan with a lot of salted water. Bring the water to a boil and then add cooking salt—about 1½ tbsp for 4 quarts, which is the quantity needed for about a pound of pasta. Slide all the pasta into the boiling water, stir with a wooden fork or spoon to separate the pieces, and cover the pan so that the water returns to a boil as soon as possible. Remove the lid and adjust the heat so that the water boils briskly, but does not boil over. The pasta is ready when it is al dente, which means that it offers some resistance to the bite. The best test to see if the pasta is ready is to fish out a piece and pop it in your mouth. It is absolutely unnecessary to add cold water to pasta after cooking, as is sometimes suggested by non-Italian cookbook writers.

The time pasta takes to cook differs according to its quality and shape, whether it is fresh or dried, and, of course, personal preference. Even in Italy a plate of spaghetti that would be perfect in Naples might be considered undercooked in Milan.

So I suggest that for store-bought dried pasta you follow the manufacturer's instructions, tasting the pasta about 1 minute before the end of the recommended cooking time, so that you can decide for yourself when it is ready. As for fresh homemade pasta, remember that it takes far less time to cook than dried pasta. Tagliatelle cook in 2–3 minutes and stuffed pasta in 4–5 minutes. This timing is calculated after the water returns to a boil.

THE AGNESI METHOD

This method of cooking factory-dried pasta was shown to me by the late Vincenzo Agnesi. I use it when I have friends to dinner since the pasta does not overcook if you leave it a minute too long in the pot. It also retains the characteristic flavor of semolina.

Bring a large saucepan of water to a boil, add sea salt to taste, then add the pasta, and stir. When the water has come back to a boil, cook for 1 minute, stirring frequently. Turn off the heat, put a tea towel over the pan, and close with a tight-fitting lid. Let sit for the same amount of time that the pasta would take to cook by the normal method, i.e. if it were still boiling, then drain and serve.

DRAINING PASTA

Pasta should be drained as soon as it is al dente (literally, "to the tooth"): you must be able to feel its texture when you bite into it. However, if the pasta is going to be cooked further, by baking or frying, drain it when it is still slightly undercooked. Pasta for salads should be even more al dente.

It is important to drain pasta properly. Use a colander that is large enough to contain all the pasta and that has feet to stand on. Tip in the pasta, give the colander two sharp shakes, and immediately turn the pasta into a heated bowl, the frying pan with the sauce, or the saucepan in which it was cooked. (It's easier to toss it in the pan without making a mess.) Gnocchi and hollow shapes need more draining since water may be trapped. However, pasta should never be overdrained, as it needs to be slippery for coating with the sauce. Do not leave it sitting "naked" in the colander. It should be dressed as soon as it is drained.

In southern Italy they do not use a colander for long pasta. The spaghetti is lifted out of the pan with two long forks. It is kept in the air for a few seconds for the excess water to run off and then immediately transferred to the pan or serving bowl. The Neapolitans say *Gli spaghetti devono avere la goccia*—"spaghetti must be still just dripping."

Homemade Pasta
MAKING THE DOUGH

1½ cups Italian Grade 00 flour
2 large eggs

Makes about 12 oz pasta,
enough for 4 people as a first
course or 3 as a main course

Note: I recommend the use of Italian Grade 00 flour for making pasta dough. It is the best for this purpose because it absorbs the eggs more evenly, is easier to knead and roll out, and, above all, makes a more fragrant, delicate pasta. Italian 00 flour is now available in most supermarkets and delicatessens.

1　Put most of the flour on the work surface and make a well in the center. Place the rest of the flour to one side. Break the eggs into the well. Beat them lightly with a fork for about 1 minute, then draw the flour in gradually from the inner wall of the well. I do this with 2 fingers because I find that gives me more control. When the eggs are no longer runny, draw in enough flour to enable you to knead the dough. At this stage you might have to add the flour you set aside, and even a little more from the bag, which you should keep at hand. You should add enough flour so that the dough is no longer sticky. (It is not possible to give the exact amount of flour needed because it depends on the absorption capacity of the eggs and the humidity of the kitchen.) Work until the flour and eggs are thoroughly amalgamated, then put the dough to one side and scrape the work surface clean. Wash and dry your hands.

Note: It is easier for a beginner to stretch a soft dough, though a dough that is too soft may stick and tear and become unmanageable. You can make a harder dough by replacing half the flour with fine semolina. This dough is difficult to work by hand, but it can be rolled out using the hand-cranked machine. It makes a pasta that is less delicate and less smooth in texture, but with a definite flavor, particularly suitable for vegetable sauces.

2　Proceed to knead the dough by pressing and pushing with the heel of your palm, folding the dough back, giving it half a turn, and repeating these movements. Repeat the movements for about 10 minutes if you are going to make your pasta by hand, or 2–3 minutes if you are going to use a machine. Wrap the dough in plastic wrap and let rest for at least 30 minutes, though you can leave it for up to 3 hours.

ROLLING OUT BY HAND

To roll out by hand you ideally need a *mattarello*—a long, thin Italian rolling pin—which is about 32 inches long and 1½ inches in diameter. If you do not have one, you must divide the dough and roll it out in 2 batches so that the circle of pasta does not become too large for your pin.

ROLLING OUT BY MACHINE

I still think the hand-cranked machine is the best machine to use, and worth every penny of its very reasonable price. This is how to proceed: Lightly dust the work surface with flour. Unwrap the dough and knead, as before, for another 2 minutes, then divide it into 4 equal parts. Take one piece of dough and carefully rewrap the others in plastic wrap.

Set the rollers of the machine to the widest opening. Flatten the piece of dough slightly, so that it nearly reaches the width of the machine. Run it through 5 or 6 times, folding the sheet over and giving it a 180° turn each time. When the dough is smooth, run the sheet, unfolded and without turning it, through all the settings, closing the rollers one notch at a time until you achieve the desired thickness. For good results it is very important that you push the sheet of dough through each setting. If the sheet tears or sticks to the machine, dust it on both sides with flour. For tonnarelli (like spaghetti, but square in diameter), stop rolling out at the third to last setting. For tagliatelle or tagliolini, stop at the second to last. For flat sheet pasta, stop at the last setting.

If the atmosphere is damp, dough rolled out too thin cannot be stuffed to make ravioli or other small shapes since, instead of drying, it becomes more and more soggy when filled with the stuffing. If you find this happening, stop rolling out at the second to last setting. Alternatively, I sometimes prefer to roll out the strip twice through the second to last setting. This makes the pasta just a little thinner, but not as thin as the last setting. Roll out the dough to the last setting only for lasagne or cannelloni.

LONG PASTA, TAGLIATELLE, FETTUCCINE, TONNARELLI, TAGLIOLINI

Lay each sheet of dough on a clean tea towel, letting about one-third of its length hang down over the edge of the work surface. Let sit until the pasta is dry to the touch and slightly leathery, but still pliable.

This process takes about 30 minutes depending on the humidity of the atmosphere and texture of the pasta, and is essential because it prevents the strands from sticking together. Feed each sheet through the broad cutters of the machine for tagliatelle or fettuccine, or through the narrow ones for tonnarelli or tagliolini

Separate the cut strands or wind them loosely around your hand to make nests. Spread them out on clean tea towels, and lightly dust them with semolina. Do not use flour, as it would be absorbed into the dough. The pasta is now ready to be cooked, or it can be dried and then stored in an airtight pan or plastic bag. Be very careful how you handle it because dried homemade pasta is very brittle and breaks easily.

LASAGNE AND CANNELLONI

Proceed immediately to cut the shapes without drying the sheets. Cut each pasta sheet into squares of about 5 x 3½ inches for lasagne, or 4 x 3 inches for cannelloni.

PAPPARDELLE

Roll out each sheet of pasta to the second-to-last notch of the hand-cranked machine. Let dry for no more than 10 minutes and then cut into ribbons about 5–6 inches long and ½-inch wide. Lay the pappardelle, not touching each other, on clean tea towels.

STUFFED PASTA SHAPES

You must get to work right away while the pasta dough is still fresh and pliable. Roll out the dough and stuff the sheets, one or two at a time, depending on the shape. Keep the remainder of the dough in plastic wrap.

Cook the little shapes immediately or leave them in the refrigerator until the next day, spread out on a clean cloth, dusted with semolina. Once dry, you can store stuffed pasta in plastic boxes layered with wax paper. Do not keep them for longer than a day or the stuffing might spoil.

Green Pasta

5 oz cooked fresh spinach, or frozen spinach, thawed and cooked for 5 minutes
2 cups Italian 00 flour
2 large eggs

Note: The only colored pasta I consider worth writing about is the traditional green pasta made with spinach. All the modern red, black, or brown pastas are gimmicks, and sometimes they spoil the flavor of the pasta. Flavor and color should be added only by the sauce.

1 Squeeze all the liquid out of the spinach with your hands. Chop it very finely with a knife. Do not use a food processor as it liquifies the spinach. Add the chopped spinach to the well in the flour together with the eggs, and knead and roll out as for normal pasta.

SAUCES FOR SHAPES

In Italy there are said to be 350 different shapes of pasta (I've never counted them!). Although you are unlikely to find such a vast number of pasta shapes outside Italy, there are now a very considerable number to choose from. In the recipes I explain which shape of pasta is usually dressed with the sauce in question, but you do not have to follow my suggestions slavishly. There are, however, certain basic rules that govern which pasta shapes should be dressed with which sauce. In general, long thin shapes are dressed with an olive oil–based sauce that allows the strands to remain slippery and separate. A typical recipe is the spaghettini with oil, garlic, and chili on page 98.

Thicker long shapes, such as ziti, tonnarelli, bucatini, or fettuccine, are best in heavier sauces containing prosciutto or bits of meat, cheese, and eggs. A prime example is the carbonara on page 123.

Medium-size short tubular pasta like ditali, orecchiette, and fusilli are perfect with vegetable sauces of any kind, these being the shapes traditionally made in southern Italy where pasta is most often combined with vegetables. See the recipe for the orecchiette with broccoli on page 103.

Penne and maccheroni and other large tubular shapes, as well as homemade shapes such as garganelli and pappardelle, are the perfect foil for a rich meat ragù and are great for use in most baked dishes. A ragù Bolognese is traditionally combined with tagliatelle (see page 112), and the choice for a northern Italian pasta al gratin (page 137) is penne.

As for the proportion of sauce to pasta, an average of 2 tbsp of well-reduced sauce per portion of pasta is a good general guide.

ARRANGEMENT OF RECIPES

The recipes in this book are grouped according to the main ingredient of the sauce. Thus tagliatelle with Bolognese sauce will be found with other recipes whose sauces are based on seafood and meat products, while spaghetti with tomato sauce is with the other recipes for vegetable-based sauces.

PASTA WITH VEGETABLE SAUCES

Pesto
PESTO SAUCE

¼ cup pine nuts
3 oz fresh basil leaves
1 garlic clove, peeled
pinch of sea salt
4 tbsp freshly grated Parmesan
2 tbsp freshly grated aged
    pecorino
⅓ cup extra virgin olive oil
3 tbsp unsalted butter

Pesto freezes very well. Omit the garlic and the cheeses and add them just before you are going to use the sauce.

Use young basil leaves for pesto; basil that has been growing for too long acquires an unpleasantly strong taste. The pine nuts must be fresh, i.e. of the current year, and the olive oil must be a very good but unassertive one. If possible, use an oil from Liguria or Lake Garda; they are less pungent than a Tuscan oil, and less herby than an oil from Puglia.

The oil must be added slowly, so as to create the right thickness. Some cooks add walnuts as well as pine nuts, but I prefer to use only pine nuts in order to keep the emphasis on the fresh flavor of the basil. If you have time, make your pesto by hand in a mortar; more juices are released than would be by the chopping action of the metal blade in a food processor or blender. I add a little softened butter to the pesto just before serving to make the sauce sweeter and more delicate. Before tossing the pesto with the pasta, always dilute it with 3 or 4 tbsp of the water in which the pasta was cooked.

1 Heat the oven to 350°F. Spread the pine nuts on a baking sheet and toast in the oven for 5 minutes or so. This will bring out the flavor of the nuts.

2 **To make in a mortar:** Put the basil leaves, garlic, cooled pine nuts, and salt in the mortar. Grind against the sides of the mortar with the pestle, crushing the ingredients until the mixture has become a paste. Mix in the grated cheeses. Add the oil gradually, beating with a wooden spoon.

To make in a food processor or blender: Cut the garlic into thin slices and drop them into the bowl of the food processor or blender. Add the basil, pine nuts, salt, and oil and process until creamy. Transfer the sauce to a bowl and mix in the cheeses.

3 Melt the butter over the lowest heat and blend into the pesto.

Trofie al Pesto
TROFIE WITH PESTO SAUCE

Serves 4 as a main course

3 small new potatoes
1¼ cups young French beans
14 oz dried trofie
pesto sauce from the previous
    recipe (page 93)

In Liguria, the motherland of pesto, potato and a handful of French beans are cooked with the pasta. I like to use trofie in this recipe, a shape traditionally served with pesto in Genoa. If you cannot find it, use fusilli.

1   Cook the potatoes in their skins in boiling salted water. Drain, then peel and slice them. Put in a bowl.
2   Trim the beans. Cook them in plenty of boiling salted water until tender and then drain. Add to the potatoes. Toss with 3 or 4 tbsp of the pesto.
3   Cook the pasta in plenty of boiling salted water until al dente. Drain, reserving a cupful of the water, and return to the pan. Add 2 or 3 tbsp of the water to the pesto.
4   Toss the pasta with half the pesto. Transfer half the pasta to a serving dish. Spoon the potato and bean mixture over the pasta and cover with the rest of the pasta. Spread the remaining pesto over the top.

Penne in Salsa di Cipolle
PENNE WITH ONION SAUCE

Serves 4 as a starter
or 3 as a main course

4 tbsp olive oil
1 lb red onions, very finely
  sliced
sea salt and freshly ground
  black pepper
½ tsp Marmite
1 tsp plain flour
¾ lb penne
1¾ tbsp unsalted butter
freshly grated Parmigiano-
  Reggiano

This is my standby sauce for pasta during the winter
when I find tomato sauce too summery and cool—it's
comforting enough for a dark, cold day.

1 Put the oil and the onions in a large sauté pan (one that has a lid),
sprinkle with salt, and cook for 10 minutes over very low heat, stirring very
often. Stir in the Marmite, cook for 1 minute, and then mix in the flour. Mix
thoroughly to incorporate the flour. Add about ½ cup boiling water and mix
until the liquid is simmering. Put the lid on the pan and cook over a very
low heat for 30 minutes or so, stirring often and adding a few tablespoons
of hot water whenever the onion mixture starts to become too dry.
2 Cook the penne in plenty of salted boiling water until al dente and,
when it's ready, drain it and then add to the onion sauce. Stir-fry for a
minute or two, then turn off the heat and mix in the butter. Mix well
until the butter has melted and then serve, passing around the cheese
in a bowl.

Pasta al Sugo
PASTA WITH TOMATO SAUCE (Version 1)

Serves 6 as a first course
or 4 as a main course

1 medium onion, very finely
   chopped
1 medium carrot, very finely
   chopped
1 celery rib, very finely
   chopped
4 tbsp olive oil
1 garlic clove, very finely
   chopped
1 small dried chili, seeded and
   chopped (optional)
1 (28 oz) can Italian plum
   tomatoes, coarsely chopped
4 parsley sprigs
1 bay leaf
1 tsp dried oregano
1 tsp sugar
sea salt and freshly ground
   black pepper
1 lb bucatini or spaghetti
freshly grated Parmesan,
   to serve

The first tomato sauce here is denser and darker than the second one because of the many sautéed vegetables. I like it best for dressing a dish of penne or bucatini, although it is suitable for most dried pasta.

1   Slowly sauté the onion, carrot, and celery in the olive oil until well softened (at least 10 minutes). Add the garlic and chili just a few minutes before you finish the *soffritto* (sautéed mixture).

2   Add the chopped tomatoes, herbs, and sugar. Season lightly with salt and pepper.

3   Simmer gently, uncovered, for 30–40 minutes, until the oil begins to separate out into small drops around the edge. Stir occasionally to prevent the sauce from sticking to the bottom.

4   Remove and discard the parsley sprigs and the bay leaf. Push the sauce through the coarsest disc of a food mill, or blitz it for a few seconds in a food processor—or leave it as it is, as I often do. Spoon the sauce back into the saucepan and keep it hot while you cook the pasta.

5   Cook the pasta in plenty of boiling salted water until al dente. Drain well and toss with the sauce. Serve at once, and pass a bowl of freshly grated Parmesan around the table.

TOMATO SAUCE (Version 2)
A simpler and fresher tomato sauce can be made in the summer when good fresh tomatoes are on the market. Peel, seed, and coarsely chop 2 lbs of ripe tomatoes and put them in a large heavy-bottomed sauté pan with 5 tbsp extra virgin olive oil, 6 smashed garlic cloves, salt and freshly ground black pepper, and a dozen trimmed fresh basil leaves or ½ tbsp dried oregano. Cook briskly for 5 minutes, stirring frequently, until a lot of the tomato water has evaporated. Remove and discard the garlic before serving. This is the classic sauce for spaghetti.

Spaghettini Aglio Olio e Peperoncino
SPAGHETTINI WITH OIL, GARLIC, AND CHILI

Serves 4 as a first course
or 3 as a main course

12 oz spaghettini (thin
 spaghetti)
sea salt
½ cup extra virgin olive oil
3 garlic cloves, sliced
1 or 2 dried chilies, according
 to taste, seeded and crumbled

This sauce differs from that in Tagliatelle with Butter and Parmesan (page 139) in a way that demonstrates the essential difference between the cooking style of northern Italy and that of the south. The aggressive flavor of this dish shows all the characteristics of Mediterranean cooking, while the delicate, but certainly not bland, tagliatelle dish epitomizes northern Italian cooking with its abundant use of butter and Parmesan. No cheese is needed for this quick, typically Neapolitan pasta.

1 Cook the pasta in plenty of boiling salted water, remembering that dried spaghettini will cook in about 6 minutes.
2 Meanwhile, put the oil, garlic, and chilies in a frying pan large enough to hold all the pasta later. Cook for 1 minute over low heat. As soon as the garlic aroma rises, the sauce is ready. Remove from the heat immediately or the garlic might burn; this would ruin the taste of the oil.
3 Drain the pasta as soon as it is al dente. Do not overcook it. Transfer the pasta immediately to the frying pan. Stir-fry for a minute or so, using two forks and lifting the pasta high into the air so that every strand is glistening with oil. Serve at once, preferably straight from the pan.

Paparele e Bisi
TAGLIATELLE WITH PEAS

Serves 6 as a first course
or 4 as a main course

4 tbsp butter
2 oz unsmoked pancetta,
 chopped
1 tbsp finely chopped onion
1½ cups cooked peas, or
 frozen petits pois, thawed
1 tbsp chopped flat-leaf parsley
½ cup chicken stock
sea salt and freshly ground
 black pepper
homemade tagliatelle made
 with 2⅓ cups Italian 00 flour
 (page 85) and 3 large eggs,
 or 1 lb Italian dried egg
 tagliatelle
2 oz Parmesan, freshly grated

Paparele and *bisi* are the Venetian words for wide tagliatelle and *piselli*, peas, which are one of the Venetians' favorite vegetables. Here they are used to dress fresh tagliatelle in a delicate, well-balanced sauce. The sauce is also suitable for dressing a dish of farfalle.

1 Put half the butter, the pancetta, and the onion in a small saucepan and sauté until the onion is soft and golden.

2 Mix in the peas and the parsley and then add the stock. Stir and add salt and pepper to taste. Cover the pan and cook over gentle heat until the peas are tender. The sauce should be quite thin.

3 Meanwhile, cook the pasta in plenty of boiling salted water until it is al dente. Drain and return to the pan.

4 Toss the pasta with the rest of the butter, pour the sauce over the top, and stir in the Parmesan.

Orecchiette con i Broccoli
PASTA WITH BROCCOLI

Serves 4 as a first course
or 3 as a main course

1 lb broccoli
sea salt and freshly ground
   black pepper
12 oz orecchiette or other
   medium-size pasta, or
   12 oz whole wheat spaghetti
2 garlic cloves, peeled
1 dried chili, seeded
3 salted anchovies, boned and
   rinsed, or 6 canned anchovy
   fillets, drained
6 tbsp extra virgin olive oil
4 tbsp freshly grated aged
   pecorino

The combination of vegetables and pasta has its origins in southern Italy. In Puglia this sauce is always served with orecchiette, which means "little ears" because of their hollow shape. Although orecchiette are made at home there, with semolina, flour, and water, they are now produced commercially by the best Italian pasta manufacturers.

I find that this sauce, as well as being good with orecchiette, is also one of the few that can stand up to the nutty flavor of whole wheat pasta (of which, like most Italians, I am not particularly fond). Whole wheat pasta is made in a number of shapes, among which spaghetti is by far the most successful.

1 Trim the broccoli. Divide into small florets and cut the stalks into 1-inch rounds.

2 Bring a large saucepan of water to a boil. Add about 1½ tbsp of salt and then add in the broccoli. Stir well and cook for 5 minutes after the water has come back to a boil. Remove the broccoli from the water with a slotted spoon and lay them on paper towels. Pat dry and set aside.

3 Bring the broccoli water back to a boil and add the pasta. Cook in the usual way until very al dente.

4 While the pasta is cooking, chop the garlic, chili, and anchovies together and sauté them in half the oil for 2 minutes, using a large frying pan. Mix in the broccoli and sauté for a few minutes, turning constantly.

5 When the pasta is done, drain, and transfer it to the frying pan. Stir-fry for 1 minute, then taste to check the seasoning.

6 Before you serve the pasta, add the rest of the olive oil and stir in the pecorino. If you like, you can serve a bowl of freshly grated Parmesan on the side, although I find that the pecorino gives the dish enough of a cheesy taste.

Tagliatelle col Sugo di Funghi
TAGLIATELLE WITH MUSHROOM SAUCE

Serves 6 as a first course
or 4 as a main course

1 oz dried porcini
1 lb mixed fresh mushrooms
5 tbsp unsalted butter
4 shallots, very finely chopped
sea salt and freshly ground
   black pepper
1 garlic clove, finely chopped
1 tbsp chopped flat-leaf parsley
1 tbsp chopped fresh marjoram,
   or 2 tsp dried marjoram
2 tsp tomato paste
1 tbsp all-purpose flour or
   Italian 00 flour
1 cup chicken stock
⅔ cup dry white wine
about ¼ of a nutmeg, grated
homemade tagliatelle,
   made with 3 large eggs
   and 2⅓ cups Italian 00 flour
   (page 85), or 1 lb Italian dried
   egg tagliatelle
freshly grated Parmesan,
   to serve (optional)

I altered an old family recipe to suit the mushrooms that are more readily available outside of Italy. There are more and more species of wild mushrooms in the shops these days, especially during autumn, the mushroom season, but they are not equally available. The other reason I adapted the Italian recipe is that the sauce is so good that I want to be able to make it at any time of the year, and not only when the wild mushrooms are in season.

The woody, leafy perfume of ceps is given here by the dried porcini, which you can easily buy in Italian delicatessens and many supermarkets. To these you add a selection of cultivated mushrooms for a sweeter flavor and for texture.

1 Put the dried porcini in a bowl and cover with very hot water. Set aside to soak for 30 minutes or so and then lift them out. If they still have some grit, rinse under cold water. Pat the porcini dry and chop them. Filter the liquid through a cheesecloth-lined sieve and reserve.
2 Clean the fresh mushrooms by wiping them with damp paper towels. If they are very dirty, rinse them under cold water. Dry and chop them coarsely. (I use a food processor, which I pulse for only a few seconds.)
3 Put half the butter and the shallots in a large sauté pan, add a pinch of salt, and cook until the shallots are soft. Stir in the garlic and herbs and sauté for another minute. Add the tomato paste and cook for 30 seconds. Add the dried porcini, sauté for 5 minutes, and then add the fresh mushrooms. Sauté over a moderate heat for 5 minutes, turning the mushrooms over and over to *insaporire*—take up the flavor. Season with a little more salt and with a generous grinding of pepper. Lower the heat and cook for another 5 minutes.

Recipe continued overleaf

TAGLIATELLE WITH MUSHROOM SAUCE

continued

4   Melt the remaining butter in a heavy saucepan and blend in the flour. Add the stock, stirring constantly and vigorously until well blended.

5   Heat the wine and add to the butter and stock mixture together with the nutmeg. Add some of the filtered porcini soaking liquid, just enough to add mushroom flavor to the sauce, but not too much because it can be overpowering. Continue cooking very gently for about 15 minutes. Stir in the mushroom mixture. Check the seasoning and cook over the lowest possible heat for about 10 minutes.

6   Meanwhile, cook the tagliatelle in plenty of boiling salted water until al dente. Drain, but do not overdrain, reserving a cupful of the water.

7   Turn half the pasta into a heated bowl and toss with half the mushroom sauce. Cover with the rest of the pasta and mix in the remaining sauce. If the pasta seems too dry, add 2–3 tbsp of the reserved water. Remember that fresh pasta absorbs a lot of liquid while it is sitting in the bowl. Serve at once with the optional cheese.

PASTA WITH MEAT & FISH SAUCES

Bucatini all'Amatriciana

BUCATINI WITH SMOKED PANCETTA AND TOMATO SAUCE

Serves 6 as a first course
or 4 as a main course

12 oz smoked pancetta cubes

1 tbsp olive oil

1 small onion, very finely
chopped

sea salt and freshly ground
black pepper

1 garlic clove, finely chopped

1 dried chili, seeded and finely
chopped

½ cup dry white wine

2 cups tomato sauce (version
2, page 96)

1 lb bucatini

6 tbsp freshly grated aged
pecorino

freshly grated Parmesan,
to serve

Amatrice is a town in the central Apennines where huge cauldrons of this dish are prepared for the local *festa* on August 15. The sauce is traditionally made with pork jowl, and seasoned with a lot of dried chili and grated pecorino to counterbalance the fattiness of the meat. I use pancetta—usually smoked—sold in cubes.

1 Put the pancetta and the oil in a nonstick frying pan and sauté until the fat has been rendered from the pancetta and the pancetta is crisp and browned. Stir frequently.

2 Add the onion and a pinch of salt to the frying pan and sauté for about 10 minutes. Mix in the garlic and chili. Cook for another minute or so and then splash in the wine. Turn the heat up and let the wine bubble away to reduce it by half. Pour in the tomato sauce and simmer for 15 minutes to allow the flavors to combine. Add salt and pepper to your liking.

3 Cook the bucatini in plenty of boiling salted water until al dente. Drain thoroughly, giving the colander a few sharp shakes so that the water trapped in the bucatini comes out. Transfer the pasta to a heated bowl and mix in three-quarters of the sauce and all the pecorino. Toss very thoroughly and then spoon the rest of the sauce over the top. Serve immediately, passing around the Parmesan separately in a bowl.

Tagliatelle al Ragù
TAGLIATELLE WITH BOLOGNESE SAUCE

Serves 6 as a first course
or 4 as a main course

2 tbsp unsalted butter
3 tbsp extra virgin olive oil
2 oz unsmoked pancetta or
   bacon, finely chopped
1 small onion, finely chopped
½ carrot, finely chopped
1 celery rib, finely chopped
1 garlic clove, finely chopped
1 bay leaf
12 oz lean chuck or braising
   beef, ground
1 tbsp tomato paste
⅔ cup red wine
⅔ cup chicken stock
2 pinches grated nutmeg
sea salt and freshly ground
   black pepper
homemade tagliatelle, made
   with 3 large eggs and
   2⅓ cups Italian 00 flour
   (page 85), or 1 lb Italian
   dried egg tagliatelle
freshly grated Parmesan,
   to serve

The early emigrants from southern Italy to the U.S. took their beloved spaghetti with them. In America, when they opened their restaurants, they realized that the locals were great meat lovers. Thus, instead of introducing spaghetti with the traditional tomato sauce, the Italians had the clever idea—financially clever, but not gastronomically—of serving spaghetti with a meat sauce or meat balls. The meat sauce was a watered-down version, both literally and figuratively, of the ragù Bolognese. It quickly caught on, and spaghetti Bolognese became synonymous with Italian cooking. But in fact there is no combination of pasta and sauce that is less typically Italian!

In Bologna, ragù is used to dress the fresh pasta—tagliatelle, not spaghetti—homemade with eggs and local soft-wheat flour. And what a wonderful dish it is. If you cannot afford the time to make your own tagliatelle, remember that dried egg tagliatelle made by a reputable Italian producer is often better than fresh store-bought pasta made with inferior flour, minimal eggs, and a lot of water.

1   To make the Bolognese sauce, heat the butter and oil in a heavy saucepan and cook the pancetta for 2 minutes, stirring constantly.

2   Add the onion, and when it has begun to soften, add the carrot, celery, garlic, and bay leaf. Cook for another 10 minutes, stirring frequently.

3   Add the ground beef and brown it as much as possible, crumbling it in the pan with a fork. Do this over a high heat so that the meat browns rather than stews.

4   Add the tomato paste and continue to cook over high heat for another 2 minutes. Still over high heat, add the wine and boil to evaporate. Remove and discard the bay leaf and pour in the stock. Season with the nutmeg, salt, and pepper. Mix well, reduce the heat, and simmer, uncovered, for about 2 hours. Stir occasionally and add a little hot water if the sauce becomes too dry. The ragù should cook very slowly indeed, at the lowest possible simmer.

5   Cook the pasta in plenty of boiling salted water. Fresh pasta cooks quickly, so stay close and test after 1½ minutes. Drain as soon as it is al dente, reserving a cupful of the pasta water.

6   Return half the pasta to the hot saucepan and stir in about half the ragù. Pour in the rest of the tagliatelle and the rest of the ragù. Mix very well, adding 2–3 tbsp of the reserved water if the pasta seems dry. Transfer to a heated bowl or deep dish and serve immediately, passing the cheese around separately.

Tagliolini Verdi col Salmone e i Funghi

GREEN TAGLIOLINI WITH A SALMON AND MUSHROOM SAUCE

Serves 3–4

¾ oz dried porcini
12 oz piece of fresh salmon
1 cup fish or vegetable stock
½ cup dry white wine
5 tbsp unsalted butter
1 shallot, very finely chopped
sea salt and freshly ground
    black pepper
6 oz cultivated fresh
    mushrooms, cleaned and
    coarsely chopped
1½ tbsp flour
3 tbsp heavy cream
homemade green tagliolini,
    made with 2 large eggs,
    2 cups Italian 00 flour,
    and 5 oz cooked or frozen
    spinach (page 89), or
    12 oz dried green tagliolini
    or tagliatelle
bunch of fresh dill, chopped
freshly grated Parmesan, to
    serve

In no way can I claim this to be a traditional Italian dish. It is an Anna Del Conte invention, good enough to pass on. It is definitely a *piatto unico* (one-course meal), with a good salad to be served afterwards, but not with it. If you cannot find dried green egg pasta, use the usual common yellow variety.

1   Put the dried porcini in a small bowl and cover with very hot water. Set aside to soak for about 30 minutes.

2   Meanwhile, put the salmon in a saucepan and cover with the stock and wine. Bring to a boil and boil for 1 minute. Remove from the heat and leave the salmon in the pan to finish cooking while you prepare the sauce.

3   Put half the butter and the shallot in a heavy saucepan. Season with a little salt and cook gently until the shallot is soft, stirring occasionally.

4   Lift the porcini out of the soaking water. If they are very dirty, rinse them under cold water. Dry and chop them coarsely. Filter the porcini liquid through a sieve lined with cheesecloth to catch any grit, and reserve.

5   Add the chopped porcini to the shallot and sauté gently for 5 minutes. Mix in the cultivated mushrooms, turn the heat up, and cook, stirring frequently, until the mushrooms have released their liquid.

6   Lift the fish out of the stock and place it on a board. Strain the stock and reserve.

7   Blend the flour into the mushroom sauce and cook for a minute or so, stirring constantly. Stir in a cupful of the fish stock and stir rapidly over very low heat until smoothly blended. Add the rest of the stock very gradually, stirring constantly. Add 2–3 tbsp of the filtered porcini liquid. The sauce should be quite thin.

8 Bring the sauce slowly to a boil, then immediately lower the heat so that only a few bubbles break the surface of the sauce every now and then, and cook for 30 minutes. I use a flame diffuser. Alternatively you can cook the sauce in a bain-marie: place the pan containing the sauce in another saucepan of gently simmering water. You can of course simmer your mushroom sauce for as little as 5 minutes, but you will not achieve the same velvety, delicate yet rich sauce. At the end of the cooking time, stir in the cream. Taste and adjust the seasoning.

9 Skin and bone the fish and flake the flesh. Add to the sauce and keep warm.

10 Cook the tagliolini in plenty of boiling salted water until al dente. Drain and return the pasta to the hot saucepan in which it cooked. Toss with the remaining butter. Transfer to a heated bowl and cover with the sauce. Sprinkle the dill over the top just before serving. Pass the grated Parmesan around in a bowl.

Tonnarelli alla Puré di Tonno
TONNARELLI WITH TUNA AND ANCHOVY PURÉE

Serves 4 as a first course
or 3 as a main course

7 oz Italian or Spanish canned
   tuna packed in olive oil,
   drained
1½ salted anchovies, boned
   and rinsed, or 3 canned
   anchovy fillets, drained
3 tbsp pine nuts
3 tbsp freshly grated Parmesan
sea salt and freshly ground
   black pepper
4 tbsp extra virgin olive oil
homemade tonnarelli, made
   with 2 large eggs and
   1⅔ cups Italian 00 flour
   (page 85), or 12 oz Italian
   dried egg tonnarelli or
   spaghetti

In some supermarkets the canned tuna for sale is skipjack, an inferior variety of the tuna fish family, smaller in size, coarser in taste, and less flavorful than the Mediterranean tuna. I strongly advise you to buy the better-quality tuna produced in France, Spain, or Italy and preserved in olive oil. It is more expensive, but it is a very superior product. And it is absolutely necessary for this delicate creamy sauce.

Tonnarelli are a kind of square homemade pasta, particularly suitable for a smooth fish sauce.

1   Put the tuna, anchovies, pine nuts, cheese, and pepper to taste in a food processor. Process while gradually adding the olive oil.
2   Slide the pasta into a saucepan of boiling water, to which only 1 tbsp salt has been added. (The sauce is quite salty.) Cook until al dente.
3   Scoop out a cupful of the pasta water and add about 6 tbsp of it to the sauce through the funnel of the processor. The sauce should have the consistency of a thin béchamel. Taste and check the pepper.
4   Drain the tonnarelli and transfer to a heated bowl. Pour the sauce over it and toss thoroughly. Serve immediately.

Pasta con le Sarde
PASTA WITH FRESH SARDINES

Serves 4 as a main course

4 tbsp currants
6 tbsp extra virgin olive oil
1 red or Spanish onion, very
  finely sliced
sea salt and freshly ground
  black pepper
4 tbsp pine nuts
7 oz wild or cultivated fennel
  fronds
1 lb fresh sardines, boned
  (see Note on page 120)
2 salted anchovies, boned and
  rinsed, or 4 canned anchovy
  fillets
1 tsp fennel seeds
12 oz bucatini

*The dish can be prepared a
few hours in advance and then
baked for an extra 15 minutes
to heat the pasta through.*

This dish from Sicily is like a history of the island on a plate: part Greek, part Saracen, part Norman. The sardines and the wild fennel, typical food of the ancient Greeks, are used here to dress the most Italian of all foods, pasta. The dressing is lightened and made more interesting by the inclusion of pine nuts and currants, a Saracen influence, and the finished dish is cooked in the oven, a method brought to the island by the Normans. If you cannot get hold of wild or cultivated fennel leaves, use a small fennel bulb, cut into strips, together with its feathery green top.

1 Soak the currants in warm water for 10 minutes. Drain and dry well with paper towels.
2 Put 2 tbsp of the oil in a frying pan, add the onion and a pinch of salt, and sauté gently for 15 minutes, stirring frequently, until soft. Mix in the currants and the pine nuts and cook for another 2 minutes.
3 Meanwhile, blanch the fennel fronds in a large saucepan of boiling salted water for 1 minute. (If you are using a fennel bulb, cook until soft.) Lift the fennel out of the water with a slotted spoon, and dry with paper towels. Reserve the cooking water. Chop the fennel and add to the onion mixture. Cook over a very low heat for 10–15 minutes, adding 2–3 tbsp of the fennel water whenever the mixture appears too dry.
4 Heat the oven to 400°F.
5 Chop about half the sardines and the anchovies and add to the pan with the fennel seeds and a generous grinding of pepper. Cook gently for 10 minutes, stirring frequently and adding more fennel water whenever necessary. Taste and adjust the seasoning.

Recipe continued overleaf

PASTA WITH FRESH SARDINES

continued

6 Heat 2 tbsp of the remaining oil in a nonstick frying pan. When the oil is very hot, but not yet smoking, slide in the remaining whole sardines and fry on both sides for 5 minutes.

7 Meanwhile, cook the pasta in the fennel water until very al dente. Drain, return the pasta to the pan, and dress immediately with the sardine sauce.

8 Grease an oven dish with a little oil and transfer the pasta to it. Lay the fried sardines over the pasta, drizzle with the remaining oil, and cover with foil. Bake for 15 minutes.

Note: To clean and bone fresh sardines, snap off the head of each fish and pull it away, thus removing most of the inside. Remove the back fin by pulling it off, starting from the tail end. Hold the sardine with one hand and open the belly with the thumb of the other hand, running it against the spine on both sides. Open the fish, butterfly-fashion, and pull the spine sharply from the head end towards the tail end, giving a last sharp tug to remove the tail. Wash and dry the boned fish.

Spaghetti alla Carbonara
SPAGHETTI WITH EGGS AND BACON

Serves 4 as a first course
or 3 as a main course

1 tbsp olive oil
4 fresh sage leaves
1 garlic clove, peeled
4 oz smoked pancetta or
  smoked bacon, cut into
  matchsticks
12 oz spaghetti
3 large eggs
6 tbsp freshly grated Parmesan
sea salt and freshly ground
  black pepper
4 tbsp unsalted butter

The creation of this dish can be attributed to the
carbonari—charcoal burners—who used to make
their charcoal in the mountainous forests of Lazio.
Traditionally, the meat used was the jowl of the pig, but
nowadays most carbonara is made with pancetta, which
is belly of pork, similar to bacon but cured differently.

1 Heat the oil, sage leaves, and garlic clove in a large frying pan. Add
the pancetta and sauté for about 10 minutes, until the pancetta is golden
brown and the fat has run out. Discard the garlic and the sage.
2 Cook the spaghetti in plenty of boiling salted water until al dente.
3 Meanwhile, lightly beat the eggs in a bowl and add the Parmesan,
a little salt, and a generous amount of black pepper.
4 Drain the pasta, reserving a cupful of the water. Return the spaghetti
to the saucepan and toss with the butter, then add to the frying pan. Stir-
fry for a minute or so.
5 Remove from the heat. Pour the egg and cheese mixture over the
spaghetti, turn off the heat, and stir thoroughly with two forks before
bringing the frying pan straight to the table.

Pappardelle con la Lepre
PAPPARDELLE WITH RABBIT

Serves 5–6 as a main course

2 tbsp olive oil

5 tbsp unsalted butter

1 oz unsmoked pancetta, chopped

1 small onion, very finely chopped

1 small celery rib, very finely chopped

1 garlic clove, finely chopped

small sprig of rosemary, finely chopped

the legs of 1 rabbit

⅔ cup red wine

2 level tsp plain flour or Italian 00 flour

⅔ cup chicken stock

sea salt and freshly ground black pepper

pinch of grated nutmeg

2 tbsp heavy cream

homemade pappardelle, made with 3 large eggs and 2⅓ cups Italian 00 flour (page 85), or 1 lb Italian dried egg pappardelle or tagliatelle

Only the legs of the rabbit are used for this dish. You can roast the saddle as they do in Tuscany, which is where this dish originally comes from. It is a rich dish, and is regarded as a *piatto unico*—one-course meal—even in Italy, where pasta is usually only the first course.

1 Heat the oil and half the butter in a sauté pan and cook the pancetta for 2 minutes, stirring constantly. Add the onion and sauté for another 5 minutes, stirring very frequently. Add the celery, garlic, and rosemary and cook until soft. Push the *soffritto* to one side of the pan.

2 Add the rabbit legs and brown well on all sides. Raise the heat, add the wine, and boil until the liquid has reduced by half.

3 Transfer the hare to a plate. Stir the flour into the cooking juices. Cook for 1 minute and then pour in half the stock. Mix well. Return the rabbit to the pan and season with salt and nutmeg. Turn the heat down to very low and cook gently for a good hour, with the lid slightly askew. If the sauce gets too dry add a little of the remaining stock. The sauce should be rather thick in the end.

4 Remove the rabbit from the pan. Bone the legs and cut the meat into very small pieces. Return the meat to the pan and add the cream and pepper to taste. Cook for about 2 minutes, stirring constantly. Taste and adjust the seasoning, then remove from the heat. Reheat the sauce before adding to the pasta.

5 Cook the pasta in plenty of boiling salted water until al dente—remember, if you are using fresh homemade pasta it will only take about 1 minute to cook. Drain and transfer the pasta into a heated bowl. Add the remaining butter and spoon over the hot rabbit sauce. Serve at once.

BAKED AND STUFFED PASTA

Ravioli di Carne
MEAT RAVIOLI

Serves 4 as a main course

For the pasta dough

2⅓ cups Italian 00 flour
  (page 85)

3 eggs

For the filling

1 tbsp olive oil

2½ oz unsmoked pancetta,
  very finely chopped

12 oz lean ground beef

⅔ cup meat stock

1 sprig of rosemary

sea salt and freshly ground
  black pepper

½ cup freshly grated Parmesan

1 egg

¼ tsp ground cinnamon

For the sauce

4 tbsp unsalted butter

2 smashed garlic cloves

6–8 fresh sage leaves, torn
  into smallish pieces

¾ cup freshly grated Parmesan

When I was a child in Milan, I loved to make ravioli. They can be filled with meat, pumpkin, spinach, or even fish. Meat ravioli were my favorite and, indeed, are the traditional—and the most popular—ravioli, served with melted butter flavored with fresh sage and garlic. Here is my family recipe.

1 First make the pasta dough (page 85) and leave it wrapped in plastic wrap while you make the filling.

2 To prepare the filling: heat the oil and pancetta in a saucepan and, after about 5 minutes, add the ground beef. Fry the meat, breaking it up with a fork so that it all gets properly browned, which will take just over 5 minutes. Pour in the stock, then add the sprig of rosemary and the salt and pepper, and cook gently for about 30 minutes. Stir frequently.

3 When the meat is cooked, discard the rosemary sprig, transfer the meat into a bowl, and let it cool for 10–15 minutes. Mix in ½ cup of the cheese, together with the egg and the cinnamon. Taste and adjust the seasoning.

4 Now start kneading the pasta dough by hand or by machine. When this is done, make the ravioli.

5 Put the pasta dough on the work surface and cut off about one-quarter, leaving the rest wrapped in plastic wrap. Roll out the dough in the pasta machine notch by notch as far as the second-to-last notch, as described on page 87. If you are rolling out by hand, roll the dough out as thin as you possibly can.

Recipe continued overleaf

MEAT RAVIOLI
continued

6 Work on one strip of dough at a time, keeping the remaining strips covered with a clean tea towel. Place mounds of the filling (about 1 tsp each) in a straight line along the length of the strip of dough, spacing them about 1½ inches apart and the same distance from the one long edge. Fold the dough lengthways over the filling and, using a pastry wheel, trim the edges where they meet. Then cut into squares between each mound of filling. Separate the squares and squeeze out any air that may be caught in the ravioli. Seal them tight with moistened fingers.

7 Place the ravioli, well separated, on clean dry tea towels. Cut off another quarter of the dough, knead in any trimmings from the previous batch, and roll the strip out as before. If you are rolling out by hand, keep the dough you are not working on well covered or it will dry up and become brittle. Continue making more ravioli until you have used up all the filling and/or all the dough. Leave the ravioli uncovered until properly dry; you can then cover them with another cloth.

8 Bring a large saucepan of water to a boil with 1½ tbsp salt. Drop the ravioli gently into the pan. (If your saucepan is not large enough, cook the ravioli in 2 batches and keep the first batch warm in an oven set to very low heat, dressed with some of the flavored butter—see step 9.) Give the ravioli a gentle stir with a wooden spoon and cook in simmering water—not fast-boiling or the ravioli might break—for 3–4 minutes until they are done. The best way to tell if they are done is to try one: the pasta should be still firm to the bite—al dente—around the edge. Lift the ravioli out with a slotted spoon and transfer them immediately to a heated and buttered bowl. Pat them dry with kitchen paper.

9 While the ravioli are cooking, make the sauce. Melt the butter in a small saucepan with the garlic and sage leaves. Fry gently until the sage leaves start to sizzle and the butter begins to turn golden. Remove and discard the garlic. Pour this simple sauce over the ravioli as soon as they are cooked and sprinkle with Parmesan. Serve at once, passing around the remaining cheese in a separate bowl.

Lasagne al Forno
BAKED LASAGNE

Serves 4–6

homemade lasagne made with
3 large eggs and 2⅓ cups
Italian 00 flour (page 85),
or 1 lb Italian dried egg
lasagne
Bolognese sauce (page 112)
1 tbsp sea salt
1 tbsp vegetable or olive oil
¾ cup freshly grated Parmesan
1 tbsp unsalted butter

For the béchamel sauce
3 cups whole milk
5 tbsp unsalted butter
½ cup flour flavored with
2 pinches of grated nutmeg
Sea salt and freshly ground
black pepper

Few dishes have been so badly copied abroad as baked lasagne, a dish that surely has acquired an appalling image. Yet when well-made, it is one of the finest creations of the very rich Bolognese cuisine. This is a party dish, perfect for a family celebration.

1 If you are making your own lasagne noodles, lay the pasta rectangles out, separate from each other, on clean tea towels.

2 While the Bolognese sauce is cooking, make the béchamel. You will find the recipe on page 137.

3 Choose a large sauté pan. Fill it with water and add the salt and oil. When the water is boiling, slide in 5 or 6 lasagne noodles at a time. Move them around with a wooden fork to keep them from sticking to each other. When they are al dente, lift them out with a slotted spatula and plunge them into a bowl of cold water. Lift out, lay on cloths, and pat dry with paper towels.

4 Heat the oven to 425°F.

5 Butter an 8 x 12-inch ovenproof dish. Spread 2 tbsp of the Bolognese sauce on the bottom. Cover with a layer of lasagne noodles and spread 2 tbsp or so of Bolognese over the pasta, followed by the same amount of béchamel sauce. Sprinkle with a little Parmesan. Repeat, building up the dish in thin layers until you have used up all the ingredients. The top layer must be béchamel.

6 Dot with the butter and bake for 20 minutes. Remove from the oven and allow to rest for at least 5 minutes before serving so the flavors have time to develop.

Il Raviolone
PASTA AND SPINACH ROLL

Serves 8 as a first course
or 6 as a main course

1½ lbs frozen leaf spinach,
  thawed, or 2¾ lbs fresh
  spinach
sea salt and freshly ground
  black pepper
3 tbsp very finely chopped
  shallots
2 tbsp unsalted butter
8 oz fresh ricotta
3 oz Parmesan, freshly grated
½ tsp grated nutmeg
1 egg yolk
homemade pasta dough, made
  with 1⅔ cups Italian 00
  flour, the yolks of 4 large
  eggs, and just enough cold
  water to help the dough
  absorb the flour (page 85)
4 large slices of unsmoked ham

For dressing the roll
6 tbsp unsalted butter, heated
  with 1 smashed garlic clove
  and 4–6 fresh sage leaves, or
  a thin béchamel sauce (see
  Note, opposite)
freshly grated Parmesan

In this dish the procedure for stuffing pasta is different. The whole sheet of pasta dough is rolled around the spinach filling. The roll is sliced when cold, just like a roast, and then heated up in the oven with its sauce. It results in a very attractive presentation.

1   If you are using frozen spinach, cook the thawed spinach in a covered pan with a little salt for 5 minutes. If you are using fresh spinach, discard any wilted or discolored spinach leaves and the tougher stalks. Wash the spinach, and then cook in a covered pan with just the water that clings to the leaves and with a little salt for 5–8 minutes, or until tender. Drain the spinach, squeezing lightly to remove most of its moisture. Set aside.

2   In a frying pan, sauté the chopped shallot in the butter over moderate heat. When the shallot turns pale gold, add the spinach and sauté for 5 minutes, turning the spinach over and over to *insaporire*—take up the flavor.

3   Transfer the contents of the frying pan to a food processor and add the ricotta, grated Parmesan, nutmeg, and, last of all, the egg yolk. Process for a few seconds. Check and adjust the seasoning.

4   Roll out the pasta dough into as thin a sheet as possible, about 20 x 14–16 inches. Lay it flat in front of you. Square the sides to make a neat rectangle.

5   Place the ham slices to cover the pasta rectangle completely, leaving a clean edge of about 1 inch on all sides.

6   Spread the spinach filling over the ham. Roll up as for a Swiss roll by first making a pleat and then rolling fairly tightly. Wrap the pasta roll tightly in cheesecloth and tie the two ends securely with string.

7   Use a fish pan or other long, deep pan that can hold the roll comfortably with about 4 quarts of water. Bring the water to a boil, add about 2 tbsp of salt, and then put in the pasta roll. Cook at a gentle but steady boil for 35 minutes.

8   Lift out the roll. Unwrap it while it is hot and set it aside to cool, when it will be easier to carve.

9 Heat the oven to 400°F.

10 Cut the roll into ½-inch slices with a very sharp knife or an electric knife. (It is easier to slice the roll when cool.)

11 Place the slices in a generously buttered shallow baking dish, overlapping them a little. You can dress the slices with either the garlic- and sage-flavored butter and then a generous amount of Parmesan, or with a layer of Parmesan covered with the thin, seasoned béchamel. Cover the dish with foil and bake for 15–20 minutes. Remove from the oven and let sit for 5 minutes before serving.

Note: For a thin béchamel, use 3 cups whole milk, 5 tbsp unsalted butter, and ⅓ cup flour. Follow the recipe on page 138, heating the milk with 1 bay leaf.

Pasta 'Ncaciata
EGGPLANT AND RIGATONI CAKE

Serves 4–5 as a main course

2 eggplants, total weight
    about 1 lb
sea salt and freshly ground
    black pepper
vegetable oil for frying
1 lb penne or rigatoni
4 tbsp unsalted butter
double quantity tomato sauce
    (version 2, page 96)
8 oz fresh mozzarella cheese,
    coarsely grated or chopped
4 tbsp freshly grated Parmesan
4 tbsp freshly grated aged
    pecorino
1 tbsp dried oregano
2 tbsp dried white breadcrumbs

This is a very showy southern Italian dish traditionally baked in a dome-shaped container, which can be tricky to unmold. In this recipe I suggest using a springform pan. This dish can be prepared a few hours in advance.

1   Cut the eggplants into ¼-inch-thick slices. Place a board on a slant over the sink. Put layers of eggplant slices on the board, sprinkling each layer with salt. Let sit to drain for 1 hour. Rinse thoroughly and pat each slice dry.

2   Heat enough oil in a large frying pan to come about 1 inch up the sides of the pan. The oil is hot enough when a corner of an eggplant slice dipped into it sizzles. Slide in a few slices of eggplant at a time and fry until deep golden on both sides. Do not overcrowd the slices or they will not fry properly.

3   Remove the fried eggplant with a slotted spoon, drain well, and place in a dish lined with paper towels.

4   Cook the rigatoni in plenty of boiling salted water until very al dente. Drain and return the rigatoni to the saucepan in which they were cooked and toss with the butter. Mix in the tomato sauce, the three cheeses, oregano, and pepper to taste. Check the seasoning.

5   Heat the oven to 375°F

6   Line the bottom of an 8-inch springform cake pan with eggplant slices. Fill in any gaps with cut-up pieces of eggplant. Line the sides of the pan with eggplant slices, cutting to fit. Place any eggplant left over on the bottom of the pan. Fill the pan with the rigatoni mixture and press down lightly. Sprinkle with the breadcrumbs.

7   Bake for 20 minutes or until the filling is hot.

8   Remove from the oven and run a knife around the side of the pan. Place a heated round serving dish over the top of the pan and turn the pan upside down. Tap the base of the pan and give the dish a sharp shake or two. Unclip the ring and lift the pan away carefully. If necessary, press into place any pieces of eggplant stuck to the pan. Allow the cake to stand for at least 5 minutes for the flavors to combine.

Pasta al Gratin
MACARONI AND CHEESE

Serves 4 as a first course
or 3 as a main course

2 oz fontina, grated
2 oz Parmesan, freshly grated
12 oz penne or macaroni

For the béchamel sauce
3 cups whole milk
5 tbsp unsalted butter
½ cup flour
sea salt and freshly ground
  black pepper
grated nutmeg

Years ago, at the beginning of my married life in England, my husband asked me what my favorite pasta dish was. "Very difficult question," I answered.

Recently, however, when he asked me the question again, I replied, "Pasta al gratin." "Oh really?" he said, and thought, "What about that discerning palate she's so proud of?" But he was thinking of the macaroni and cheese of his school days, and I was thinking of the velvety, cheesy delight of Pasta al Gratin.

Although it is made with a sauce with a French name, the dish is Italian. It is made in many regions, with certain variations. In the north, for instance, Parmesan is used, sometimes mixed with Emmental or fontina, as in my recipe, while in Naples a buffalo mozzarella is cut up and pushed here and there among the penne.

For all its simplicity, Pasta al Gratin needs a careful and patient cook, able to make a velvety béchamel and to drain the pasta at the right time, i.e. when still slightly undercooked, so that it can reach the right texture during baking.

1   To make the béchamel sauce, heat the milk until hot but not boiling. Remove from the heat.

2   Melt the butter, remove the saucepan from the heat, and stir in the flour. Put the pan back on the heat and cook, stirring constantly, for about 30 seconds.

Recipe continued overleaf

MACARONI AND CHEESE
continued

3 Remove the pan from the heat and add the milk gradually. At the beginning add only a couple of tablespoons and incorporate well before adding another few tablespoons. Adding the milk slowly in this way helps prevent the flour from forming lumps. Return the pan to the heat and cook until the sauce comes to a boil. Season with salt and pepper and with a generous grating of nutmeg. Cook for a few minutes, stirring constantly.

4 To finish the sauce you can either use a flame diffuser under the pan or a bain-marie. Leave the sauce to cook very, very gently for 10–15 minutes; you need to stir only occasionally. This long, slow cooking makes a rich, velvety sauce that you would not be able to achieve if you cooked the béchamel for a shorter time, that is, just enough to cook the flour.

5 Add the cheeses to the béchamel. Taste and adjust the seasoning.

6 Cook the pasta in plenty of boiling salted water until very al dente. Drain thoroughly (penne tend to hold water in their hollows).

7 Heat the oven to 350°F.

8 Coat a shallow baking dish (about 2 inches deep) with a little of the sauce. Dress the pasta with about two-thirds of the béchamel and transfer to the prepared dish. Spread the rest of the sauce all over the top. Bake for about 30 minutes, until the penne at the top begin to brown.

9 Let sit for 5 minutes before serving to allow the flavors to blend while cooling a little.

OTHER FAVORITES

Tagliatelle al Burro e Formaggio
TAGLIATELLE WITH BUTTER AND PARMESAN

Serves 4 as a first course
or 3 as a main course

homemade tagliatelle, made
    with 2 large eggs and
    1⅔ cups Italian 00 flour
    (page 85), or 14 oz Italian
    dried egg tagliatelle
sea salt
2 oz Parmesan, freshly grated,
    plus extra for serving
4 tbsp best-quality unsalted
    butter

In my home in Milan when I was a child, we used special butter for this sauce. The highest quality farm butter was sold, cut in pieces and wrapped in muslin, by the best delicatessen in Via Monte Napoleone. And the tagliatelle were, of course, homemade.

This recipe is characteristic of northern Italian cooking. It is also the sauce used when you are lucky enough to have a white truffle to shave over it. To do the dish justice, you should make your own pasta and buy the best unsalted butter, as well as making sure your Parmesan is a proper Parmigiano-Reggiano, of which you grate an ample quantity over the dish just before serving.

1 Cook the pasta in plenty of boiling salted water until al dente. Drain—but do not overdrain—and turn half the pasta into a heated serving bowl. Add about 4 tbsp of the cheese and stir well.
2 Cut the butter into small pieces and add half to the bowl. Toss thoroughly, then add the remaining cheese. Add the remaining butter and toss until all the butter has melted. Serve at once and top with more grated cheese.

Tagliolini Piccanti Freddi
TAGLIOLINI WITH A PIQUANT SUN-DRIED TOMATO SAUCE

Serves 4 as a first course

10 oz sun-dried tomatoes in
   olive oil, drained
6 tbsp extra virgin olive oil
1 or 2 dried chilies, according
   to taste, strength, and size,
   seeded and crumbled
5 garlic cloves, smashed
12 fresh basil leaves, torn into
   small pieces
homemade tagliolini made with
   2 large eggs and 1⅔ cups
   Italian 00 flour (page 85),
   or 10 oz Italian dried egg
   tagliolini or spaghetti
sea salt
2½ oz black olives, such as
   Kalamata

This is the best room temperature pasta dish I know, and it has always been a great success at my demonstrations. When I do not have the time or the inclination to make my tagliolini, I prefer to buy the best brand (which usually means the most expensive) of Italian dried tagliolini or tagliatelle.

1   Cut the sun-dried tomatoes in thin strips and put them in a bowl large enough to hold the pasta later. Add the oil, chilies, garlic, and basil.
2   Cook the tagliolini in plenty of boiling salted water. Drain it when it is even more al dente than you would like for eating it hot. (Overcooked cold pasta is really unpleasant.) Turn the pasta into the bowl and toss very thoroughly, lifting the strands up high so as to separate them. Let sit for 2 hours or so for the flavors to infuse, then fish out the garlic and discard. Scatter the olives over the pasta and serve.

Linguine e Zucchine al Sugo di Pistacchio e Basilico
LINGUINE AND ZUCCHINI WITH A PISTACHIO AND BASIL SAUCE

Serves 6 as a first course
or 4 as a main course

¾ cup extra virgin olive oil, preferably from Sicily or Puglia
4 garlic cloves, smashed
1⅓ lbs zucchini, cut into matchsticks
sea salt and freshly ground black pepper
4 oz shelled pistachios
2 cups fresh basil
1 cup fresh flat-leaf parsley
16 oz dried linguine
1 tbsp unsalted butter

I first had this dish many years ago at a dinner party in a friend's house overlooking Catania, in Sicily. It remains high on the list of my favorite pasta dishes and I think its presentation and the combination of flavors epitomize the very best of Sicilian cooking. This sauce is also perfect for dressing a dish of farfalle.

1 Heat 2 tbsp of the oil and the garlic in a nonstick frying pan. When the oil is hot, add the zucchini and fry at a lively heat until golden all over. Shake the pan very often. The zucchini is ready when tender, not still crunchy but not yet soft, and when the flavor has fully developed, about 15 minutes. Season with salt and pepper.

2 While the zucchini is frying, put the pistachios into a small saucepan. Cover with water, bring to a boil, and boil for 10 seconds. Skin the pistachios, taking them out of the hot water a few at a time for easier peeling. Dry them thoroughly and put in a food processor.

3 Rinse and dry the basil and parsley and add to the pistachios. Process while adding the rest of the oil through the funnel. Stop the machine, push the mixture down from the side of the bowl, and process again a few seconds. Add salt and pepper to taste. Scoop out the mixture into a serving bowl and place the bowl in a warm oven.

4 Cook the pasta in plenty of salted boiling water until al dente. Drain, reserving a cupful of the pasta water, and turn immediately into the heated bowl. Add the butter and toss very thoroughly, adding 3 or 4 tbsp of the reserved water to loosen the sauce.

5 Spoon the zucchini and its juices over the top of the pasta and serve at once.

Conchiglie di Radicchio Rosso col Ripieno di Pasta

RED RADICCHIO LEAVES FILLED WITH PASTA

Serves 4 as a first course

generous bunch of flat-leaf
   parsley, stalks removed
1 garlic clove
2 salted anchovies, boned and
   rinsed, or 4 canned anchovy
   fillets, drained
1 fresh green chili, seeded and
   cut into thin matchsticks
4 tbsp extra virgin olive oil
sea salt
8 oz ditali or gnocchi
4 outer leaves from a large
   head of red radicchio
freshly ground black pepper
   (optional)

Years ago, I read this short clip in The Times (London), which I shall always remember:

Laurette Bruuson threw macaroni salad at Richard, her groom, during a tiff at their wedding reception in Tampa, Florida, and he responded by shooting her with a .22 pistol.

I am not particularly fond of cold pasta salads but I doubt I would go that far, and I certainly wouldn't if I were eating this pasta salad, which I find particularly good. I use a peppery oil for this dish, such as an extra virgin oil from Chianti or a fruity and herby oil from Sicily or Puglia.

1 Chop the parsley, garlic, and anchovies and put them in a large bowl together with the chili matchsticks. Beat in the oil and add salt to taste.
2 Cook the pasta in plenty of boiling salted water, remembering that cold pasta needs to be more al dente than hot pasta. Drain, refresh under cold water, and drain again thoroughly. Pat dry with paper towels. Transfer the pasta to the bowl with the dressing and toss well. Let sit for about 2 hours for the flavors to infuse.
3 Wash and dry the radicchio leaves thoroughly and lay them on individual plates. Taste and add pepper, if you desire. Fill the salad leaves with the pasta just before serving.

Spaghettini con le Cappe Sante
SPAGHETTINI WITH SCALLOPS

Serves 3-4

12 oz spaghettini (thin
  spaghetti)
sea salt
8 scallops
½ cup extra virgin olive oil
2 garlic cloves, very finely
  chopped
2 tbsp chopped flat-leaf parsley
½ tsp dried chili flakes
1 cup dried white breadcrumbs
sea salt

A quick and easy recipe which needs only perfect timing. You want the pasta and the scallop sauce to be ready at the same time for combining in the final stir-fry. Do not add the scallops to the *soffritto*—frying mixture—until the pasta is almost done, because they will get tough if cooked for longer.

1 Cook the spaghettini in a large saucepan of salted boiling water.
2 While the pasta is cooking, clean the scallops, washing and drying them. Then separate the white meat from the coral and cut into ¾-inch pieces.
3 Heat the oil in a large frying pan and add the garlic, parsley, and chili flakes. Stir-fry for 1 minute and then throw in the breadcrumbs. Fry, stirring the whole time, for another minute to get the crumbs nice and golden all over before you add the white part of the scallops. Fry for another 30 seconds, by which time the pasta should be ready.
4 Drain the spaghettini, add to the frying pan, and mix the ingredients together. Fry the whole thing for 1 minute, then add the coral and give it a final stir-fry of 1 minute. Serve immediately straight from the frying pan.

RISOTTI

AND MORE

Risotto is a relative newcomer to the Italian culinary scene, where most dishes can trace their origins back to the Renaissance, if not to Roman times. It was only during the nineteenth century that risotto became popular in the northern regions of Italy—Piedmont, Lombardy, and Veneto—where the rice was cultivated, as indeed it still is.

A genuine risotto, for all its apparent simplicity, is a challenge to most cooks. Although there are certain rules to observe, the feel of making a good risotto can only be learned with practice. The first essential is to use top-quality ingredients. Secondly, one must remember that risotto is prepared according to a well-defined method. It is not just a mixture of rice and other ingredients, and it is certainly not, as some people have believed, a dish that Italians make from an assortment of leftovers. Rice is often the only ingredient, apart from flavorings. When there are other ingredients, they are almost always cooked with the rice, so as to allow the flavors to combine and fuse.

The rice must be medium-grain white rice, which absorbs the liquid in which it cooks and which swells up without breaking or becoming mushy. Only two types of rice are suitable for making risotto: superfino and fino. Arborio, which is widely available, is the most popular variety of superfino rice and is suitable for all risotti. It has large plump grains with a delicious nutty taste when cooked. Carnaroli, a new superfino variety, is produced in relatively small quantities. It keeps its firm consistency, while its starch dissolves deliciously during the cooking. Vialone Nano, a fino rice, has a shorter, stubbier grain containing starch of a kind that does not soften easily in the cooking. It is my favorite rice for vegetable risotti. Vialone Nano cooks more quickly than Arborio—it takes 15 minutes, as opposed to 20 minutes for Arborio. Both Carnaroli and Vialone Nano can be found in specialty Italian shops. In most of the recipes, I have specified the best variety of rice to use, bearing in mind availability.

The choice of saucepan is crucial to the success of the dish. The pan must be wide, heavy-bottomed, and large enough to contain the rice when it has finished cooking, by which time it will have almost tripled its volume. Ideally it should also be round-bottomed, to prevent the rice from sticking in the corners.

The quality of the stock is also very important. It should be made with meat, chicken, or vegetables, or top-quality stock cubes or powder. Italian stock for risotto is never made with lamb or pork. Vegetable stock is particularly suitable for a vegetable or seafood risotto; for the latter a light fish stock is also good. If you do not have any stock already prepared, use high-quality meat stock cubes; there are some on the market that do not contain monosodium glutamate. Good Italian rice takes about 15–20 minutes to cook, according to the variety. At the end of the cooking the rice should be al dente—firm but tender without a chalky center—and the risotto should have a creamy consistency.

You will find here recipes for eleven risotti, many with vegetables, others with seafood or meat. These last ones are more nourishing and are definitely main course dishes, while the lighter risotti with vegetables can be the start, all'Italiana, of any dinner party.

Risotto should be eaten as soon as it is done, but if you do not like to cook when your guests have already arrived, you can make a timballo instead, and accompany it with a suitable sauce. For this, keep the risotto slightly undercooked, being careful to add the stock very gradually at the end of the cooking or the rice will be too liquid when it is ready. Spread the risotto out on a large dish and leave it to cool.When it is cold, spoon it into a ring mold that has been generously buttered and sprinkled with dried breadcrumbs.

Set the mold in a bain-marie and bake in a 425°F oven for about 20 minutes. Loosen the risotto all around the mold with a knife. Place a large round platter over it and turn the whole thing upside down. Give the mold a few taps on the top, shake the platter and mold vigorously, and lift the mold away. If some of the risotto sticks to the mold, remove it and patch the shape up neatly. Nobody will notice, especially if you place some basil or parsley over it.

Risotto al Limone
RISOTTO WITH LEMON

Serves 4 as a first course
or 3 as a main course

6 cups chicken or vegetable
stock
4 tbsp unsalted butter
1 tbsp olive oil
2 shallots, very finely chopped
1 celery rib, very finely
chopped
2½ cups Italian rice,
preferably Arborio
½ organic lemon
5 or 6 fresh sage leaves
leaves from small sprig of
fresh rosemary
1 egg yolk
4 tbsp freshly grated Parmesan
4 tbsp heavy cream
sea salt and freshly ground
black pepper

This recipe first appeared in my book *Secrets from an Italian Kitchen*. Friends and reviewers alike have all said they found it one of the best risotti ever, which is why I feel no qualms about including it in this book.

1 Bring the stock to a gentle simmer (keep it simmering all through the cooking of the rice).
2 Heat half the butter, the oil, shallots, and celery in a heavy-bottomed saucepan and sauté until the *soffritto*—frying mixture—of shallot and celery is softened (about 7 minutes). Add the rice and continue to sauté, stirring, until the rice is well coated with the fats and is partly translucent.
3 Pour in about ⅔ cup of the simmering stock. Stir very thoroughly and cook until the rice has absorbed nearly all of the stock, still stirring. Add another ladleful of simmering stock, and continue in this manner until the rice is ready. You may not need all the stock. Good-quality Italian rice for risotto takes 15–20 minutes to cook.
4 Meanwhile, thinly pare the zest from the lemon half and chop it with the herbs. Mix into the rice halfway through the cooking.
5 Squeeze the lemon half into a small bowl and combine it with the egg yolk, Parmesan, cream, a little salt, and a very generous grinding of black pepper. Mix well with a fork.
6 When the rice is al dente, remove the pan from the heat, and stir in the egg and cream mixture and the remaining butter. Cover the pan and let rest for 2 minutes or so. Then give the risotto an energetic stir, transfer to a heated dish or bowl, and serve at once, with more grated Parmesan in a little bowl if you wish.

Risotto alla Milanese
RISOTTO WITH SAFFRON

Serves 4–5 as a first course
or as an accompaniment

6½ cups chicken or meat
stock
1 small onion, very finely
chopped
5 tbsp unsalted butter
1¾ cups Italian rice,
preferably Carnaroli
¾ cup good red wine
½ tsp powdered saffron or
saffron strands crushed to a
powder
sea salt and freshly ground
black pepper
¾ cup freshly grated Parmesan

Some Italians have queried the use of red wine instead of white in this recipe. My answer is that not only in my own family—Milanese for generations—but in some very authoritative cookbooks the suggested wine is red. Other recipes do not include any wine, but add some cream or milk at the end. The choice is yours.

As for the saffron, the strands are definitely more reliable than the powder, but they must be added earlier in the cooking so as to dissolve well, thus losing some flavor during the cooking.

This is the risotto traditionally served with *osso buco* and with *cotolette alla Milanese*, breaded veal cutlets.

1 Bring the stock to simmering point (keep it at a very low simmer all through the cooking of the rice).
2 Put the onion and 4 tbsp of the butter in a heavy-bottomed saucepan and sauté until soft and translucent. Add the rice and stir until well coated with fat. Sauté until the rice is partly translucent. Pour in the wine and boil for 1 minute, stirring constantly, and then pour in ⅔ cup of the simmering stock. Cook until nearly all the stock has been absorbed and then add another ladleful of the simmering stock. Continue cooking and adding small quantities of stock, keeping the risotto at a steady lively simmer all the time. If you finish the stock before the rice is properly cooked, add a little boiling water.
3 About halfway through the cooking (good rice takes 15–20 minutes to cook), add the saffron dissolved in a little stock. When the rice is al dente, taste and adjust the seasoning.
4 Remove the pan from the heat and mix in the rest of the butter and 4 tbsp of the Parmesan. Put the lid on and let sit for 1 minute or so. When the butter and the Parmesan have melted, give the risotto a vigorous stir and transfer to a heated dish. Serve immediately, with the rest of the cheese passed around separately.

Risotto al Pomodoro
RISOTTO WITH TOMATOES

Serves 4 as a first course
or 3 as a main course

1½ lbs ripe tomatoes, peeled
7 tbsp extra virgin olive oil
3 or 4 garlic cloves, thickly
   sliced
good handful of fresh basil
   leaves, torn into pieces
6 cups vegetable stock
1½ cups Italian rice,
   preferably Carnaroli
sea salt and freshly ground
   black pepper

The match of risotto with tomatoes is a modern one, but it is so good that I am sure it will become a classic. This risotto does not contain any butter. It is very light and fresh, and it is very good, if not better, at room temperature.

1   Cut the peeled tomatoes in half. Squeeze out and discard some of the seeds. Chop the tomatoes coarsely and put them in a heavy-bottomed saucepan large enough to hold the rice later. Remember that the rice will be nearly three times its original volume by the end of the cooking.

2   Add 4 tbsp of the oil to the pan, then add the garlic and half the basil. Cook briskly for 1–2 minutes, stirring.

3   Meanwhile, bring the stock to a simmer (keep it simmering very gently all through the making of the risotto).

4   Add the rice to the pan with the tomatoes and cook for about 2 minutes, stirring constantly.

5   Stir in a ladleful of simmering stock and continue cooking, adding more stock little by little and stirring until the rice is al dente. If you want to serve the risotto at room temperature, remove it from the heat when the rice is slightly underdone; it finishes cooking as it cools.

6   Add salt and pepper to taste and mix in the rest of the oil. Transfer to a serving dish and sprinkle the remaining basil leaves on the top. If you serve the risotto at room temperature, fluff it up with a fork before bringing it to the table.

Risotto al Peperone
RISOTTO WITH PEPPERS

Serves 4 as a first course
or 3 as a main course

2 large peppers, preferably
  1 yellow and 1 red
2 tbsp unsalted butter
4 tbsp extra virgin olive oil
2 garlic cloves, sliced
4 tbsp chopped flat-leaf parsley
4 tomatoes, peeled, seeded, and
  chopped
6 cups vegetable stock
1½ cups Italian rice, preferably
  Arborio or Vialone Nano
4 pinches of chili powder
sea salt and freshly ground
  black pepper
12 fresh basil leaves

Risotto, the staple of northern Italy, never used to be made with olive oil, the cooking fat of the south. The advantage of butter is that, when melted, it penetrates into the grains of the rice, which is what you want to happen, while oil makes a film around them. But some modern risotti are now made with a mixture of butter and oil, especially when oil is the ideal dressing for the accompanying ingredient—peppers in this case. This is my adaptation of a traditional risotto from Voghera, a town in southwest Lombardy that is famous for its peppers.

1   Wash and dry the peppers. Cut them into quarters and remove and discard the seeds, cores, and white ribs. Cut them into thin strips about ¾-inch wide. Set aside.
2   In a heavy-bottomed saucepan heat the butter and 2 tbsp of the oil. Throw in the garlic and half the parsley and, when they begin to sizzle, add the strips of pepper and cook for 5 minutes. Mix in the chopped tomatoes and continue cooking for another 5 minutes, stirring frequently.
3   Meanwhile, in a separate saucepan bring the stock to a simmer.
4   Add the rice to the *soffritto*—frying mixture—and cook, stirring the whole time, for a minute or two. Now begin to add the simmering stock gradually, a ladleful at a time. Wait to add each subsequent ladleful until the previous one has nearly all been absorbed.
5   When the rice is almost done, season with the chili powder and salt and pepper to taste. Remove the pan from the heat and stir in the remaining 2 tbsp of oil and the remaining parsley. Transfer to a heated deep serving dish, sprinkle with the basil leaves, and serve at once.

Risotto alla Paesana
RISOTTO WITH VEGETABLES

Serves 4 as a first course
or 3 as a main course

½ cup shelled fresh peas
8 oz asparagus
3½ oz zucchini
8 oz ripe firm tomatoes,
  peeled, or Italian canned
  plum tomatoes, drained
4 tbsp extra virgin olive oil
bunch of fresh flat-leaf parsley,
  chopped
1 garlic clove, chopped
sea salt and freshly ground
  black pepper
6 cups chicken or vegetable
  stock
2 tbsp unsalted butter
2 shallots, chopped
1¼ cups Italian rice,
  preferably Carnaroli or
  Arborio
5 tbsp dry white wine
½ cup freshly grated Parmesan
12 fresh basil leaves, torn
  into pieces

This lovely fresh risotto is best made in the spring, when the new peas and asparagus are in season. The vegetables can be varied: Put in a little celery and carrot when there is no asparagus; French beans are suitable too. Try to match the flavors of the vegetables so as not to have a strident note.

1 Cook the fresh peas in lightly salted boiling water until just tender. Meanwhile, trim and wash the asparagus and cook in boiling salted water until al dente. Drain and cut the tender part of the spears into small pieces. (Reserve the rest for a soup.) Blanch the zucchini for 2–3 minutes, then drain and cut into small cubes. Cut the tomatoes in half, squeeze out the seeds, and then cut into short strips.

2 Put half the oil, the parsley, and garlic in a sauté pan and sauté for 1 minute. Stir in all the vegetables, season lightly with salt, and sauté over a low heat for 2 minutes for them to take the flavor of the *soffritto*—the fried mixture. Set aside.

3 Heat the stock in a saucepan until just simmering (keep it simmering all through the cooking of the rice).

4 Put the rest of the oil and half the butter in a heavy-bottomed saucepan. Add the shallots and sauté until tender. Add the rice and stir to coat with the fats, then cook for 2 minutes or until partly translucent. Add the wine and boil rapidly to evaporate, stirring constantly. Add a ladleful of simmering stock and let the rice absorb it while you stir constantly. Continue to add the stock gradually, stirring frequently, until the rice is al dente. (This will take 15–20 minutes.)

5 Halfway through the cooking, stir in the vegetables with all their cooking juices. Season with pepper; taste to check the salt.

6 When the rice is done, remove the pan from the heat and add the rest of the butter, cut into small pieces, and the Parmesan. Cover the pan and let stand for a couple of minutes. Then stir vigorously and transfer to a heated dish. Garnish with the basil leaves and serve at once.

Risotto al Finocchio
RISOTTO WITH FENNEL

Serves 4–5 as a first course
or 3–4 as a main course

2 fennel bulbs, about 1⅓ lbs
   total
1⅓ tbsp olive oil
4 tbsp unsalted butter
1 small onion, finely chopped
1 celery rib, finely chopped
6 cups vegetable stock
sea salt and freshly ground
   black pepper
1½ cups Italian rice,
   preferably Vialone Nano
6 tbsp dry white wine
4 tbsp heavy cream
½ cup freshly grated Parmesan

Vegetable risotto is one of the great strengths of Venetian cooking. Of all of them, this fennel risotto is my favorite, especially when I can get hold of fennel that is full of flavor and not "the commercial variety grown in Italy for export which is beautiful but dumb" as the late Jane Grigson so aptly put it.

1 Cut off and discard the fennel stalks, but keep some of the feathery fronds. Remove any bruised outer leaves and cut the bulbs lengthwise in half. Slice the halves very finely across. Wash thoroughly and drain.

2 Put the oil, half the butter, the onion, and celery in a medium sauté pan. Sauté until the vegetables are pale gold. Add the sliced fennel and stir it over and over to let it take up the flavor. Add about 4 tbsp of the stock and cover the pan. Cook, stirring occasionally, for about 20 minutes, or until the fennel is very soft. Mash it with a fork to a purée over a high heat, so that the excess liquid evaporates. Add salt to taste.

3 Bring the remaining stock to a gentle simmer (keep it simmering all through the cooking of the rice).

4 Heat the remaining butter in a heavy-bottomed saucepan. When the butter foam begins to subside, mix in the rice and stir to coat the grains thoroughly. Sauté for a couple of minutes until the rice is partly translucent. Turn the heat up and add the wine. Let it bubble away, stirring the rice constantly.

5 Now begin to add the simmering stock a ladleful at a time. When nearly all of the first ladleful has been absorbed, add another, always stirring the rice. If you run out of stock before the rice is done, add some boiling water and continue the cooking.

6 Halfway through the cooking of the rice, stir in the mashed fennel with all the cooking juices.

7 When the rice is al dente, remove the pan from the heat and add the cream, Parmesan, and a generous grinding of pepper. Mix everything together well. Transfer to a heated dish, scatter the snipped fennel fronds over the top, and serve at once.

Risotto coi Peoci
RISOTTO WITH MUSSELS

Serves 4 as a first course
or 3 as a main course

4 lbs mussels
1¼ cups dry white wine
4 tbsp chopped flat-leaf parsley
6 tbsp olive oil
3 shallots, very finely chopped
sea salt and freshly ground
   black pepper
4 cups light fish or vegetable
   stock
1 celery rib, with the leaves if
   possible
1 garlic clove
½ dried chili, crumbled
1½ cups Italian rice, preferably
   Carnaroli or Arborio

I have always found a risotto with mussels to be rather unsatisfactory, because you either have only risotto in your mouth, albeit fishy tasting, or else a large mussel. So one day I came up with the idea of chopping up most of the mussels so that morsels of them could be enjoyed in each mouthful. This is the recipe I developed and it works very well.

1 First clean the mussels. Scrape off the barnacles, tug off the beard, and scrub thoroughly with a stiff brush under running water. Throw away any mussel that remains open after you have tapped it on a hard surface.

2 Put the wine in a large sauté pan, add the mussels, and cover the pan. Cook over high heat until the mussels are open, which will only take 3–4 minutes. Shake the pan every now and then.

3 As soon as the mussels are open, remove the meat from the shells and discard the shells. Strain the cooking liquid through a sieve lined with cheesecloth, pouring it slowly and gently so that the sand will be left at the bottom of the pan.

4 Set aside a dozen of the nicest mussels; chop the rest and put in a bowl. Mix in the parsley.

5 Pour the oil into a heavy-bottomed saucepan. Add the shallots and a pinch of salt and sauté until the shallots are soft and just beginning to color.

6 In another saucepan, bring the stock to a simmer (keep it simmering all through the cooking of the rice).

7 Meanwhile, chop the celery and garlic together. Add to the shallots with the chili. Sauté for another minute or so. Now add the rice and stir to coat with oil, then cook it for a couple of minutes until partly translucent. Pour into the mussel liquid and stir well. When the liquid has been absorbed, add the simmering stock, one ladleful at a time. Stir constantly at first. When the rice is nearly cooked, mix in the chopped mussels, then continue cooking until al dente.

8 Season with salt, if necessary, and pepper. Transfer to a heated dish and garnish with the reserved whole mussels.

Risotto con le Animelle
RISOTTO WITH SWEETBREADS

Serves 4 as a main course

1 lb lamb sweetbreads
½ organic lemon
sea salt and freshly ground
    black pepper
6 cups chicken stock
8 tbsp unsalted butter
2 shallots, finely chopped
about 8 fresh sage leaves,
    snipped
1½ cups Italian rice,
    preferably Arborio
6 tbsp dry white wine
4 tbsp Marsala (Madeira or
    port can also be used)
¾ cup freshly grated Parmesan

In restaurants, sweetbreads are often accompanied by boiled rice. That rather boring presentation has, however, led me to devise this dish, where the winey-syrupy sweetbreads are combined with a classic *risotto in bianco*.

During the truffle season, a small white truffle shaved over the top of the risotto makes the dish truly sensational.

1 Soak the sweetbreads in cold water for at least 1 hour. Rinse them and put them in a pan with the lemon half and 1 tsp of sea salt. Cover with fresh cold water and bring to a boil. Boil for 2 minutes. Drain well, plunge into cold water, and drain again. Remove all fat, white tubes, and hard bits. Put the sweetbreads between two plates with a weight on top to squeeze out all excess liquid. Dry them and cut them into morsels.
2 Heat the stock to a simmer (keep it simmering through the cooking of the risotto).
3 Melt half the butter in a heavy-bottomed saucepan. Add the shallots, four of the sage leaves, and a pinch of salt and cook until the shallots are soft and translucent.
4 Add the rice and stir to coat with butter, then sauté for 2–3 minutes until partly translucent. Pour in the white wine and boil for a minute or two until it has evaporated, stirring constantly. Now begin to add simmering stock, little by little, in the usual way. Do not add too much at one time or the risotto will not cook properly. Keep the heat lively and constant.
5 Meanwhile, melt half the remaining butter in a sauté or frying pan. Add the rest of the sage leaves. When the sage begins to sizzle, slide in the sweetbreads and sauté for 2 minutes, turning them over to brown on all sides. Add the Marsala to the pan and let it bubble away on low heat. Cook for 7–8 minutes, stirring occasionally.

6 When the rice is nearly done, pour the sweetbreads and all the juices into the risotto pan. Stir thoroughly. Taste and adjust the seasoning, and finish cooking the risotto.

7 When the rice is al dente, remove the pan from the heat. Add the remaining butter and a couple of spoonfuls of the Parmesan. Cover the pan tightly and let the butter melt for a minute or so, then stir the risotto gently but thoroughly. Transfer to a heated dish and serve at once, passing around the rest of the Parmesan in a bowl.

Risotto con le Sogliole
RISOTTO WITH DOVER SOLE

Serves 4 as a main course

5 tbsp unsalted butter
2 tbsp very finely chopped
  shallot
sea salt and freshly ground
  black pepper
6 cups light fish stock
1¾ cups Italian rice,
  preferably Carnaroli
½ cup dry white wine
2 tbsp chopped fresh dill
12 oz skinless Dover sole fillets
4 tbsp freshly grated Parmesan

It might seem extravagant to use Dover sole in a humble dish such as a risotto, but I assure you that it is necessary. You only need a small amount of Dover sole, and it does make a great difference to the dish. The delicacy and firm texture of the fish is in perfect harmony with the soft creaminess of the risotto; none of the other ingredients disturbs this happy balance of flavors.

1 Heat 4 tbsp of the butter and the shallot in a heavy-bottomed saucepan. Add a pinch of salt and sauté until the shallot is soft and translucent.

2 Meanwhile, heat the fish stock in another saucepan to simmering (keep it at the lowest simmer all through the cooking of the risotto).

3 Add the rice to the shallot and stir to coat with butter, then sauté for a minute or so until partly translucent. Add the wine and let it bubble away, stirring constantly.

4 Add about ⅔ cup of simmering stock, stir well, and let the rice absorb the liquid. Continue adding stock little by little until the rice is nearly done, then mix in half of the dill and continue the cooking.

5 Meanwhile, heat the remaining butter in a nonstick frying pan. Cut the fish fillets in half, lengthwise. Slide them into the butter and sauté for 3 minutes. Turn them over and sauté for another minute. Sprinkle with salt and pepper.

6 When the rice is al dente, mix in the Parmesan and the juices from the fish fillets. Turn into a heated dish. Place the fish fillets neatly over the top and sprinkle with the remaining dill. Serve immediately.

Risotto con la Salsiccia
RISOTTO WITH SAUSAGE

Serves 4 as a first course
or 3 as a main course

12 oz luganega sausage or
 other pure pork, coarse-
 grained Italian sausage
2 tbsp olive oil
1 sprig of fresh sage
⅔ cup full-bodied red wine,
 such as barbera
6 cups chicken stock
3 tbsp unsalted butter
2 or 3 shallots, depending on
 size, finely chopped
1½ cups Italian rice, preferably
 Arborio or Carnaroli
sea salt and freshly ground
 black pepper
freshly grated Parmesan, to
 serve (optional)

Some recipes for this dish, originally from Monza (now a suburb of Milan), suggest cutting the sausage in chunks and cooking it separately. In this case the sausage is also served separately and is added to the plated risotto by each diner. But in the following recipe, which I prefer, the fried sausage is added to the rice in the middle of the cooking so that the flavors of both ingredients blend thoroughly. You need good 100% pure pork sausage.

1 Skin the sausage and crumble it. Heat 1 tbsp of oil and the sage in a nonstick frying pan. Add the sausage and fry briskly for 5 minutes, stirring constantly. Add the wine, bring to a boil, and cook for about 5 minutes, just long enough for the sausage meat to lose its raw color.
2 While the sausage is cooking, bring the stock to a simmer (keep it just simmering through the cooking of the rice).
3 Heat the butter and remaining oil in a heavy-bottomed saucepan. Add the shallots and fry gently until soft and translucent—about 7 minutes.
4 Add the rice to the shallot *soffritto* and cook for 1–2 minutes, stirring constantly, until the grains are partly translucent.
5 Add the simmering stock a ladleful at a time. Wait to add another ladleful until the previous one has nearly all been absorbed.
6 Ten minutes after you start adding the stock, add the sausage and its juice to the rice. Stir well and continue cooking until the rice is al dente. Check the seasoning and serve at once, with the Parmesan handed around separately if you wish.

Risotto alla Scozzese
RISOTTO WITH SMOKED SALMON AND WHISKEY

Serves 4 as a first course
or 3 as a main course

4 tbsp unsalted butter
4 tbsp finely chopped shallot
sea salt
6 cups chicken or vegetable
   stock
1½ cups Italian rice, preferably
   Carnaroli
4 tbsp Scotch whiskey
8 oz smoked salmon, cut into
   ¾-inch pieces
5 tbsp heavy cream
2 tbsp chopped fresh dill
cayenne pepper
freshly grated Parmesan,
   to serve

I love smoked salmon and, like most Italians, am not averse to an occasional glass of whiskey. So here I have combined these two very Scottish ingredients with a favorite dish from my home country. It is a particularly successful match. The Parmesan is not necessary, but I think its flavor goes well with that of the smoked salmon.

1 Put the butter in a large, heavy-bottomed saucepan. Add the chopped shallot and a pinch of salt; this will release the moisture from the shallot, thus preventing it from browning. Sauté until soft and translucent, about 7 minutes.

2 Meanwhile, in another saucepan heat the stock to a simmer (keep it simmering through the cooking of the rice).

3 Add the rice to the shallot and stir to coat with butter, then cook for a couple of minutes, stirring constantly, until partly translucent. Add the whiskey and let it bubble away, stirring constantly. Add a ladleful of simmering stock and cook the rice on a lively heat, adding a ladleful of stock whenever the rice begins to get dry.

4 When the rice is al dente, add the smoked salmon, cream, dill, and cayenne pepper to taste. Mix thoroughly and check the salt before you transfer this delicious risotto to a heated dish. Serve at once, passing the cheese separately in a bowl for those who want it.

Timballi e Pasticci di Riso
MOLDED AND BAKED
RICE DISHES

I have included two molded rice recipes for this type of rice preparation. They are particularly suited to dinner parties, since they can be made in advance and then baked in the oven. They are dishes that need a more experienced cook, able to judge the exact cooking time of the different ingredients, and to shape and unmold the rice. A good point, however, is that cooked rice is very malleable. Should you find yourself with a *timballo tombé*, you can reshape the rice with your hands and nobody will know.

Torta di Risotto e Porri con la Salsa di Cozze
LEEK RISOTTO CAKE WITH MUSSEL SAUCE

Serves 6 as a first course
or 4 as a main course

2 lbs mussels
1 tbsp olive oil
2 garlic cloves
1 thick slice of lemon
12 oz leeks
6 cups vegetable stock
8 tbsp unsalted butter
2¼ cups Italian rice,
    preferably Vialone Nano
1¼ cups dry white wine
sea salt and freshly ground
    black pepper
butter and dried breadcrumbs
    for the dish
1 shallot, finely chopped
¼ tsp saffron strands

Leeks and mussels are complementary flavors. The rice here brings them together and gives substance to this dish. It is a fabulous dish for a party, well worth the time and effort.

1 Scrub the mussels in a sink full of cold water, knocking off the barnacles, and tugging off the beard. Rinse in several changes of cold water until the water is clean and no sand is left at the bottom of the sink. Discard any mussel that remains open after you have tapped it against a hard surface.

2 Put the oil, garlic, and slice of lemon in a large sauté pan. Add the mussels, cover the pan, and cook over high heat until the mussels are open, about 4 minutes. Shake the pan very often.

3 Remove the mussel meat from the shells. Discard the shells and any mussel that remains closed. Pour the mussel liquid into a measuring cup. Do it slowly so that you leave any sandy debris at the bottom of the pan. Set aside.

4 Cut off the green part of the leeks. Choose the best green leaves, wash them, and blanch in boiling water for 2–3 minutes. Drain and cut into ½-inch strips. Set aside.

5 Cut the white part of the leeks into very thin pieces. Wash thoroughly, then drain and dry them.

6 Heat the stock in a saucepan until simmering (keep it simmering all through the making of the risotto).

7 Heat the oven to 350°F.

8 Heat 4 tbsp of the butter and the white part of the leeks in a large heavy-bottomed saucepan. Sauté until the leeks are just soft and then mix in the rice. Sauté the rice until it is well coated with butter and the grains are partly translucent—about 2 minutes—and then add half the wine. Boil briskly for 1 minute, stirring constantly.

9 Add a ladleful of the simmering stock and stir well. As soon as nearly all the stock has been absorbed, add another ladleful of stock. Continue cooking the rice in this manner until it is very al dente, about 15 minutes. Mix in 2 tbsp of the butter. Taste and check the seasoning.

10   Very generously butter an 8-inch soufflé dish or cake pan and coat it with the breadcrumbs. Spoon the risotto into it, press down gently, and place in the oven while you prepare the sauce.

11   Put the shallot and remaining 2 tbsp butter in a saucepan and sauté for 5 minutes.

12   Meanwhile, pound the saffron in a mortar. Add 2–3 tbsp of the mussel liquid, stir thoroughly, and add to the shallot together with the remaining wine and mussel liquid. Bring slowly to a boil, and boil until reduced by about half. Add the mussels, stir, and check the seasoning. You might have to add a little salt, and you will need to add a lot of pepper. Cover the pan and remove from the heat.

13   Remove the risotto and loosen it from the mold with a knife. Turn the mold over onto a heated round platter, tap and shake, and then lift it off. Drape the strips of leek greens over the risotto at regular intervals. Spoon a little of the mussel sauce over the top and pour the rest into a heated bowl. Serve immediately.

Anello di Risotto di Verdure
VEGETABLE RISOTTO RING

Serves 4–6

5–6 cups vegetable stock
1 cup French beans
3½ tbsp unsalted butter
4 tbsp extra virgin olive oil
3 shallots, chopped
large bunch flat-leaf parsley,
   chopped
2 garlic cloves, chopped
1½ cups risotto rice
5 oz dry white wine
1 cup fresh peas, shelled, or
   frozen peas, thawed
½ cup freshly grated
   Parmesan cheese
3 tbsp mascarpone
sea salt and freshly ground
   black pepper
butter and breadcrumbs for
   the mold

This is a very attractive dish that can be made in advance and reheated in a hot oven for 15–20 minutes. Serve the risotto ring accompanied by the tomato sauce (version 2) from page 96 in the spring or the mushroom sauce from page 116 in the autumn. You will need a ring mold with a 1-quart capacity.

1 Heat the stock to simmering. Maintain its simmer until ready to be added to the rice. Add the beans and cook for 5 minutes. Remove from the stock and cut them into ¼-inch pieces.

2 Heat the butter and oil in a large, heavy saucepan. When the butter has melted, add the shallots. Sauté for 10 minutes, then add 2 tbsp chopped parsley and the garlic. Sauté for 2–3 minutes, stirring frequently. Add the rice and cook for 1 minute, stirring constantly. Pour in the wine, let it reduce for 1–2 minutes, then pour in one ladleful of the simmering stock.

3 Continue cooking for 10 minutes, gradually adding the stock. Mix in the peas, if you are using fresh peas, and cook for 4 minutes, then add the French beans and the frozen peas if you are using those. Continue cooking until the rice is nearly done. Mix in the Parmesan and mascarpone and salt and pepper to taste. Set aside for at least half an hour.

4 Heat the oven to 340°F. Very generously butter the ring mold and spread the breadcrumbs all over its surface. Shake off excess crumbs.

5 Spoon the risotto into the mold, pressing it down to eliminate any air bubbles. Place the mold into a roasting tin and pour some boiling water into the tin, about two-thirds up the side of the mold. Cover with foil and place the tin in the oven. Cook for 20 minutes (longer if the risotto was cold) and then remove the mold from the tin and put straight in the oven without the bain-marie. Cook for another 10–15 minutes.

6 When the risotto is ready, remove it from the oven and loosen it from the mold by running a palette knife around the edges between the mold and the risotto. Put a large, round dish over the top, turn the mold over, say a prayer, and lift off the ring mold. A ring of beautiful risotto should be sitting on the dish.

7 Fill the ring hole with the sauce and serve the rest of the sauce alongside. Sprinkle with the remaining parsley.

Risi Asciutti e Minestre di Riso
RICE AND VEGETABLE DISHES AND RICE SOUPS

The first two recipes in this section are for dishes that are somewhere between a soup and a risotto. The rice is boiled in the stock in which the vegetables are cooking; thus, the dishes are definitely not risotti. This method of cooking ensures that the taste of the vegetables predominates over the flavor of the rice.

The last three recipes are for soups, all from my hometown, Milan, the motherland of good soups. Rice soup is very popular, and can vary from a rich, earthy minestrone to a sophisticated soup with chicken, rice, and almonds floating in a pale blond pool—a very Chinese-looking soup.

Riso con le Verdure
RICE WITH VEGETABLES

Serves 6 as a first course
or 4 as a main course

1 large waxy potato, diced
2 carrots, diced
1 large leek, white and green
    part, cut into rounds
½ cup shelled fresh peas or
    green beans, according to
    season
1 celery rib, diced
1 eggplant, diced
sea salt and freshly ground
    black pepper
1½ cups Italian rice, preferably
    Vialone Nano
½ cup extra virgin olive oil
3 garlic cloves, finely chopped
12 fresh sage leaves, chopped
2 large ripe tomatoes, peeled,
    seeded, and coarsely chopped
4 oz Italian fontina or raclette,
    diced
6 tbsp freshly grated Parmesan

Northern and southern Italy meet happily in this dish, which was given to me by the Neapolitan owner of a superb greengrocer in Valtellina, an Alpine valley north of Milan. The dish is halfway between a minestrone and a risotto with vegetables and yet it tastes different than both. The flavor of the vegetables comes through strongly, enhanced by the final *soffritto*.

1 Choose a large pot—I use my earthenware stockpot with a 5-quart capacity. Put all the washed and cut vegetables (except the tomatoes) in it and add enough water to come three-quarters of the way up the side of the pot. Season with salt, bring to a boil, and simmer, uncovered, for 20–25 minutes.

2 Add the rice to the vegetables, stir well, and cook for about 15 minutes, or until done. The vegetables should be nice and soft and the rice should be al dente, thus giving a pleasing contrast of texture.

3 While the rice is cooking, make a little soffritto (frying mixture). Heat the oil, garlic, and sage in a small frying pan until the sage begins to sizzle and the garlic is fragrant. Add the tomatoes and cook for 5 minutes, stirring occasionally.

4 When the rice is ready, drain the contents of the stockpot very well (you can keep the liquid for a soup) and transfer the rice and vegetable mixture, a ladleful at a time, into a serving bowl. Dress each ladleful with a couple of spoonfuls of the soffritto, a handful of cheese cubes, a generous grinding of pepper, and a spoonful of Parmesan. Mix very thoroughly after each addition, and serve at once.

Note: By dressing the dish gradually you make sure that the soffritto and the cheese are equally distributed.

Risi e Bisi
RICE WITH PEAS

Serves 4–6 as a first course

1 small onion, very finely
   chopped
3 tbsp unsalted butter
1 tbsp olive oil
1½ lbs young fresh peas, podded
6½ cups chicken stock
1¼ cups Italian rice, preferably
   Vialone Nano
1 tsp fennel seeds, crushed,
   or 2 tbsp chopped flat-leaf
   parsley
¾ cup freshly grated Parmesan
sea salt and freshly ground
   black pepper

The Venetians' love of rice and peas is sublimated in this, the most aristocratic of rice dishes. It was served at the Doge's banquets on the feast of San Marco, on April 25, when the first young peas—grown on the islands of the Venetian lagoon—appear in the market. This is the old recipe, in which fennel seeds are used instead of parsley. The best rice to use for the dish is Vialone Nano.

1 Put the onion, half the butter, and the oil in a heavy-bottomed saucepan and sauté until the onion is pale golden and soft. Mix in the peas and cook over a low heat for 10 minutes, adding a few spoonfuls of stock during the cooking.

2 Meanwhile, bring the remaining stock to a boil in another saucepan.

3 Add the rice to the peas and sauté for 2 minutes, turning the rice over and over until the grains are partly translucent. Now add the boiling stock. Stir well and bring back to a boil. Simmer gently, stirring occasionally, until the rice is al dente. You might have to add a little more stock during the cooking.

4 A few minutes before the rice is done, add the fennel seeds or parsley, the rest of the butter, and 4 tbsp of the Parmesan. Taste and add salt and pepper to your liking. Stir thoroughly and finish cooking, then serve at once with the rest of the cheese handed around separately.

Riso e Lenticchie
RICE WITH LENTILS

Serves 4–5

4 tbsp olive oil

1 small onion, very finely
  chopped

2 oz smoked pancetta, cut into
  tiny pieces

1 small carrot

1 large celery rib

1 sprig of fresh rosemary,
  about 2 inches long

1 garlic clove

sea salt and freshly ground
  black pepper

1 rounded tsp tomato paste

6½ cups vegetable stock, or
  2 vegetable stock cubes
  dissolved in the same
  amount of water

1 cup green lentils, rinsed and
  drained

1 cup Italian rice, preferably
  Vialone Nano

extra virgin olive oil for the
  table, a Tuscan or Roman oil

This is an earthy, nourishing soup, which I first had one lunchtime in Rome at a busy, bustling trattoria opposite the Quirinale. It was the most lively place imaginable, crowded with civil servants enjoying good, homey Roman food.

1 Heat the oil, onion, and pancetta in a heavy-bottomed saucepan. (I use an earthenware pot when I cook beans.) Sauté for about 7 minutes, stirring frequently. The onion must become soft but not browned.

2 Finely chop the carrot, celery, rosemary leaves, and garlic together. Add to the onion *soffritto*—frying mixture—and cook on low heat for about 10 minutes. Stir frequently. Season with salt and stir in the tomato paste. Cook for another minute.

3 Meanwhile, heat the stock in a separate saucepan.

4 Add the lentils to the vegetable mixture. Stir well and let them *insaporire*—take up the flavor—for a minute or two.

5 Pour enough stock into the pan to cover the lentils by about 2 inches. Cover the saucepan and cook until the lentils are soft, not al dente. It is difficult to say how long that will take since it depends on the quality and freshness of the lentils. Usually lentils are ready within 1 hour. Check the liquid occasionally and add more stock whenever the lentils are too dry.

6 Add the rest of the stock and bring back to a boil. Stir in the rice and, if necessary, add more boiling stock. If you have used all the stock, pour in boiling water. The amount of liquid needed varies with the quality of the lentils, the kind of rice used, and the temperature at which the soup is cooked. The resulting soup should be quite thick: lots of rice and lentils in a little liquid.

7 Season with lots of pepper, and simmer until the rice is al dente (15–20 minutes).

8 Taste and adjust the seasoning. Serve the soup right away, passing around a bottle of extra virgin olive oil for everyone to pour a little over his serving of soup. Although not essential, I recommend this last *battesimo*—christening—because the oil livens up the earthy soup with its fruity flavor.

Minestra di Riso, Mandorle, e Prezzemolo

RICE, ALMOND, AND PARSLEY SOUP

Serves 4

¾ cup peeled almonds
6 cups chicken stock
1 chicken breast on the bone
⅔ cup Italian rice, preferably
   Vialone Nano
3 tbsp chopped flat-leaf parsley
sea salt and freshly ground
   black pepper

No clear soup like this can be successful without the basis of a good stock. If you don't have some chicken stock ready in the freezer, you can make it with a good-quality chicken bouillon cube, of which there are quite a few on the market.

This is a delicate soup to be given to people who appreciate the balance of good ingredients.

1   Heat the oven to 425°F.
2   Place the almonds on a baking tray and bake for 10 minutes, or until fragrant and golden. Chop them to the size of grains of rice.
3   In a large saucepan heat the stock until boiling. Add the chicken breast and cook gently for 10 minutes. Lift the breast out of the stock and place on a board. Add the rice to the stock and mix in.
4   While the rice is cooking, skin and bone the chicken breast and cut the meat into small strips.
5   When the rice is nearly done, stir in the chicken strips, almonds, and parsley and continue cooking until the rice is ready. Taste and add salt, if necessary, and pepper. Ladle the soup into hot bowls.

Minestrone alla Milanese
VEGETABLE SOUP WITH RICE

Serves 6

2 tbsp olive oil

2 tbsp butter

4 oz unsmoked pancetta, or
  unsmoked bacon, chopped

2 onions, coarsely chopped

4 or 5 fresh sage leaves,
  snipped

1 tbsp chopped flat-leaf parsley

2 garlic cloves, chopped

2 carrots, diced

2 celery ribs, diced

2 potatoes, about 8 oz total,
  diced

4 oz green beans, cut into
  ¾-inch pieces

8 oz zucchini, diced

8 oz Italian canned plum
  tomatoes with their juice

sea salt and freshly ground
  black pepper

8 oz Savoy cabbage, cut into
  strips

¾ cup Italian rice, preferably
  Semifino Padano or Vialone
  Nano

14 oz canned borlotti beans,
  drained

freshly grated Parmesan,
  to serve

This is the classic minestrone with rice, where rice is the starchy nourishment added to a vegetable soup. Minestrone is even better made a day in advance and warmed up. In the summer it is delicious chilled, though not straight from the fridge.

1 Heat the oil and butter in a stockpot or a large saucepan, add the pancetta, and sauté for 2 minutes. Add the onions, sage, and parsley and fry gently for 5 minutes or so.

2 Mix in the garlic, carrots, celery, and potatoes and fry for 2 minutes. Add the green beans and zucchini and sauté for another couple of minutes.

3 Cover with 10 cups of hot water and add the tomatoes and salt and pepper to taste. Cover the pan and cook at a very low simmer for at least 1½ hours. Minestrone can be cooked for as long as 3 hours and it will be even better. Don't worry that the vegetables will break down; they do not.

4 About 30 minutes before you want to eat, add the cabbage and cook for 15 minutes. Then add the rice and the canned beans and stir well. Continue cooking uncovered at a steady simmer until the rice is al dente. Serve with a bowl of Parmesan on the side.

Ripieni e Insalate di Riso
RICE STUFFINGS AND SALADS

Two recipes for rice stuffings hardly do justice to an array of dishes in which rice is the primary ingredient of the stuffing. But I have chosen my favorites.

While rice is commonly used as a filling for vegetables, its use in stuffing seafood is less common. The recipe for squid stuffed with rice is very interesting and very good; in fact, it is my preferred way of stuffing squid.

The versatility of rice is boundless. It even makes excellent salads, which is more than can be said for pasta. I have also included in this section two of my favorite recipes for rice salads.

Pomodori Ripieni di Riso
TOMATOES STUFFED WITH BASIL-FLAVORED RICE

Serves 4 as a first course

1 lb ripe tomatoes, all the
  same size
sea salt and freshly ground
  black pepper
½ cup Italian rice, preferably
  Vialone Nano
2 garlic cloves, finely sliced
12 fresh basil leaves, thinly
  sliced
1 egg
½ cup extra virgin olive oil

The rice in this recipe is not cooked prior to stuffing the tomatoes; it is simply given a long soak in the flavorful oil. By the end of the cooking the tomatoes are very soft and meld with the rice, rather than being separate containers.

1 Wash and dry the tomatoes. Cut them in half horizontally. Scoop out some of the seeds and discard. Scoop out all the pulp and the juice with a pointed spoon, taking care not to break the skin. Chop the pulp and put it in a bowl with the juice.

2 Sprinkle the insides of the tomato halves with salt and refrigerate for at least 30 minutes.

3 Add the rice to the bowl together with the garlic and basil.

4 Beat the egg very lightly and mix thoroughly into the rice mixture. Add the oil, reserving 1 tbsp, and plenty of pepper and salt to taste. Mix again very well and let sit for at least 3 hours.

5 Heat the oven to 375°F.

6 Oil a large baking dish and place the tomato halves in it, cut side up. Fill them with the rice mixture, to come level with the top of each tomato. Drizzle the remaining oil over the top of the tomatoes, cover the dish with foil, and bake until the rice is cooked, about 45–55 minutes. Serve hot.

Calamari Ripieni di Riso
SQUID STUFFED WITH RICE

Serves 3–4 as a main course

4 large squid, about 2 lbs
6 tbsp olive oil
4 tbsp cooked Italian rice,
   preferably Vialone Nano
3 tbsp chopped flat-leaf parsley
2 garlic cloves, chopped
½–1 dried chili, chopped
grated zest of ½ organic lemon
2 salted anchovies, boned and
   rinsed, or 4 canned anchovy
   fillets, drained
sea salt and freshly ground
   black pepper
½ cup dry white wine

Rice, a staple of the north, is sometimes used in fish dishes in Puglia, the heel of the Italian boot, this dish is cuttlefish, although I use squid, which are more easily available.

1   Ask your fishmonger to clean the squid, or do it yourself by following these instructions. Hold the sac in one hand and pull off the tentacles with the other hand. The contents of the sac will come out, too. Cut the tentacles above the eyes. Squeeze out the thin bony beak in the center of the tentacles. Peel off the skin from the sac and the flap. Remove the translucent backbone from inside the sac and rinse the sac and tentacles under cold water. Keep the sacs whole.

2   Cut the tentacles into small pieces and then chop them coarsely until they are about the same size as the grains of rice.

3   Put 2 tbsp of the oil in a sauté pan. Add the rice, chopped tentacles, parsley, garlic, chili, and lemon zest and sauté briskly for a few minutes to *insaporire*—let the mixture take up all the flavors.

4   Finely chop the anchovy fillets and stir into the mixture. Cook at a lower temperature for a minute or so. Taste and add salt and pepper, if necessary.

5   Heat the oven to 350°F.

6   Fill each squid sac with the rice mixture. Do not pack the stuffing too tight or the sac will burst during the cooking. Sew up the opening with a needle and thread and lay the squid in a single layer, close to each other, in an oven dish. (I use a metal pan since metal transmits heat better than ceramic.)

Recipe continued overleaf

SQUID STUFFED WITH RICE

continued

7 Pour the rest of the oil and the wine over the squid. Cover the oven dish tightly with a piece of foil and bake for about 1 hour, until the squid are tender when pricked with a fork.

8 When they are done, transfer the squid to a carving board and let cool for 10 minutes. Slice off a very thin strip from the sewn end to the thread. Cut each sac into 1-inch thick slices. If you have one, use an electric carving knife, which will make this slicing very easy. Otherwise see that your knife is very sharp. Gently transfer the slices to a serving dish.

9 Taste the cooking juices. If bland, boil briskly until reduced and full of flavor. Spoon over the squid. You can serve the dish hot, warm, or at room temperature, which I personally prefer.

Riso e Ceci in Insalata
RICE AND CHICKPEA SALAD

Serves 4

5 oz dried chickpeas, or 14 oz
   canned or organic chickpeas
   (in cartons)
sea salt and freshly ground
   black pepper
1 tsp baking soda
1 tbsp flour
1 small onion, cut in half
1 celery rib, cut in half
2 sprigs of fresh rosemary
4 fresh sage leaves
a few parsley stalks
2 garlic cloves
7 tbsp extra virgin olive oil
1 cup Italian rice, preferably
   Vialone Nano or Semifino
   Padano
1 garlic clove, finely chopped
a lovely bunch of fresh flat-leaf
   parsley, finely chopped
8 oz best ripe tomatoes, peeled
   and seeded
12 fresh basil leaves, thinly
   sliced

It is surprising how two ingredients as modest as rice and chickpeas can produce, when mixed together, such a good and attractive dish.

Cook the chickpeas properly until they are fully tender. Like my compatriots, I find nothing more unpleasant than undercooked beans. The rice should be al dente, not because of the overpraised "contrast of texture," but simply because rice is good al dente. Chickpeas, however, are good when soft. I usually use dried chickpeas, which I soak overnight before cooking. These are far better than the canned ones. But should you prefer to cut out the soaking and cooking, I suggest you use organic chickpeas.

1 Put the chickpeas in a large bowl and cover with plenty of cold water. Mix the salt, baking soda, and flour with a little cold water to make a paste and stir this into the soaking water. This helps to tenderize the skin as well as the chickpeas themselves. Let soak for at least 18 hours; 24 is better.

2 Rinse the chickpeas and put them in a pot. (An earthenware stockpot is the best for cooking beans because of earthenware's heat-retaining properties.) Add the onion and celery and cover with water to about 3½ inches over the chickpeas. Place the pot on the heat.

3 Tie the rosemary, sage, parsley stalks, and whole garlic cloves in a small piece of cheesecloth to make a bundle and add to the pot. Bring to a boil, then lower the heat and cook, covered, until the chickpeas are ready, about 2–3 hours. The liquid should simmer rather than boil. Add salt only when they are nearly done, as the salt tends to make the skin crack and wrinkle.

Recipe continued overleaf

RICE AND CHICKPEA SALAD

continued

4 Drain the chickpeas (you can keep the liquid for a bean or vegetable soup). Fish out and discard the onion, celery, and herb bag. Transfer the chickpeas to a bowl and toss, while still hot, with 2 tbsp of the oil.

5 Cook the rice in plenty of boiling salted water. Drain when just al dente. Mix into the chickpeas.

6 Put the rest of the oil, the chopped garlic, and chopped parsley in a small frying pan. Sauté for 2 minutes, stirring constantly.

7 Dice the tomatoes and mix into the *soffritto*—frying mixture. Cook for 1 minute and then spoon over the rice and chickpea mixture. Add the fresh basil and plenty of pepper. Toss thoroughly but lightly. Taste and check the salt. Serve at room temperature.

Insalata di Riso con Mozzarella ed Acciughe

RICE SALAD WITH MOZZARELLA AND ANCHOVY FILLETS

Serves 4 as a first course

1¼ cups Italian rice,
   preferably Vialone Nano
sea salt and freshly ground
   black pepper
6 tbsp extra virgin olive oil
2 hard-boiled eggs
5 oz buffalo mozzarella, cut
   into small cubes
6 salted anchovies, boned
   and rinsed, or 12 canned
   anchovy fillets, drained
4 tbsp chopped flat-leaf
   parsley
1 small garlic clove, very
   finely chopped
1 small dried chili, seeded and
   crumbled
12 black olives
1 tbsp capers, rinsed and dried

I strongly recommend using buffalo mozzarella for this dish. If possible, dress the rice 2 hours before serving.

1   Cook the rice in plenty of boiling salted water until just al dente. (Remember that when served cold, rice is better if a touch undercooked.) Drain the rice, rinse under cold water, and drain again. Transfer the rice to a bowl and pat dry with paper towels. Add 2 tbsp of the oil and set aside to cool.

2   Chop the eggs and add to the rice, together with the mozzarella.

3   Chop the anchovy fillets and place in another bowl. Mix in the parsley, garlic, and chili. Beat in the remaining oil with a fork until the sauce thickens. Season with salt and pepper to taste.

4   Spoon this dressing into the rice and mix very thoroughly with two forks so as to separate all the grains. Taste and adjust the seasoning to your liking. Scatter the olives and capers over the salad and serve at room temperature.

Risi Dolci
SWEET RICE DISHES

These last three rice recipes do not originate from the
northern regions of Italy as all the previous ones do.
The rice cake and rice fritters are from Tuscany and the
Black Rice Pudding is, oddly enough, from Sicily.

Torta di Riso
RICE CAKE WITH ALMONDS AND RAISINS

Serves 8

3 cups whole milk
1 cup superfine sugar
strip of organic lemon zest,
   yellow part only
1-inch piece of vanilla bean
2-inch piece of cinnamon stick
sea salt
⅓ cup Italian rice, preferably
   Arborio
4 tbsp raisins
2 tbsp dark rum
⅔ cup blanched almonds
4 large eggs, separated
grated zest of ½ organic lemon
butter and dried breadcrumbs
   for the pan
confectioner's sugar, to finish

*This is the Florentine version
of a cake that is popular all
over central Italy. I make it
with Arborio rice, as it swells
during the cooking while
absorbing the milk. You can
add other ingredients to taste,
such as chocolate pieces and/
or candied peel. It is a firm
yet moist cake that is equally
delicious with or without a
dollop of thick cream on top.
It should not be served until
at least a day after making, to
allow the flavors to blend.*

1 Put the milk, 3 tbsp of the sugar, the strip of lemon zest, the vanilla bean, the cinnamon stick, and a pinch of salt in a saucepan and bring to a boil. Add the rice and stir well with a wooden spoon. Cook, uncovered, over very low heat for about 35 minutes, stirring frequently, until the rice has absorbed the milk and is soft. Set aside to cool.

2 Heat the oven to 350°F.

3 Put the raisins in a bowl and pour in the rum. Let them sit to plump up.

4 Spread the almonds on a baking sheet and toast them in the oven for about 10 minutes, or until they are quite brown. Shake the tray occasionally to prevent them from burning. Let the almonds cool slightly, then chop them coarsely.

5 Remove the strip of lemon zest, the vanilla bean, and cinnamon stick from the rice and spoon the rice into a mixing bowl. (Wash and dry the vanilla bean so that you can use it again.) Add the egg yolks, one at a time, mixing well after each addition. Add the remaining superfine sugar, the almonds, the raisins with the rum, and the grated lemon zest to the rice and egg mixture and mix everything together thoroughly.

6 Whisk the egg whites until they are stiff, then fold them gently into the rice mixture.

7 Butter an 8-inch springform pan. Line the bottom with parchment paper and then butter the paper. Sprinkle with breadcrumbs to coat evenly and shake out the excess crumbs.

8 Spoon the rice mixture into the prepared tin. Bake in the oven (still at the same temperature) for about 45 minutes, or until a wooden skewer inserted in the middle of the cake comes out just moist. The cake should also have shrunk a little from the sides of the pan.

9 Let the cake cool in the pan, then remove the sides and turn the cake over onto a plate. Remove the base of the pan and the parchment paper. Place a round serving platter on the cake and turn it over again. Let sit for at least 24 hours before serving the cake. Sprinkle with sifted confectioner's sugar before serving.

Riso Nero
BLACK RICE PUDDING

Serves 6

2½ cups whole milk
⅓ cup Italian rice
½ cup superfine sugar
⅔ cup blanched almonds,
  chopped
pinch of sea salt
pinch of ground cinnamon
⅔ cup black coffee
1¾ oz bittersweet chocolate
  (70% cocoa solids), finely
  chopped or grated
grated zest of 1 small organic
  orange
1 tbsp unsalted butter
⅔ cup whipping cream

This is one of the few Sicilian contributions to the vast range of Italian rice sweets. It is different from the rice desserts of the central Italian regions—the motherland of rice cakes and puddings—because it contains a high proportion of chocolate and coffee. In Sicily this dish is served without cream, but even though I am not a cream fan, I must admit that cream lightens the almondy chocolate flavor of the riso nero.

1   Put the milk, rice, sugar, almonds, salt, cinnamon, and coffee in a heavy-bottomed saucepan. Bring to a boil and simmer until the rice is very soft, about 1 hour, stirring frequently. If you use a flame diffuser, you can leave it a little longer, but be careful because the milky rice tends to stick to the bottom of the pan.
2   Remove the pan from the heat and mix in the chocolate and the orange zest.
3   Grease a 2-quart glass bowl or pudding mold with the butter. Spoon in the rice mixture and let cool. When cold, cover with plastic wrap and put in the fridge to chill.
4   Free the pudding all round with a thin knife and turn it out onto a round platter.
5   Whip the cream and spread it all over the brown dome just before serving.

Frittelle di Riso
RICE FRITTERS

Serves 4

2½ cups whole milk

pinch of sea salt

⅓ cup Italian rice, preferably Semifino Padano or Vialone Nano

2 tbsp sugar

pared zest of ½ organic orange, in strips

pared zest of ½ organic lemon, in strips

2 large eggs

vegetable oil for frying

confectioner's sugar, to decorate

These fritters are sold and eaten in the streets of Florence and other Italian towns as a *merenda*—snack—and they are absolutely delicious. You can easily make them yourself and try to capture the atmosphere of an Italian vacation.

1 Put the milk, salt, rice, sugar, and fruit zest in a heavy-bottomed saucepan. Bring slowly to a boil, stirring frequently. Cook, uncovered, at a very low heat for about 1 hour, or until the rice has absorbed all the milk and is very soft. Stir frequently. Spoon the mixture into a bowl and let cool a little.

2 Lightly beat the eggs, then incorporate into the rice mixture. Mix very well and then refrigerate. If possible, chill for 1 hour so the mixture firms, which will make it easier to shape and fry.

3 Heat the oil to 340°F in a wok or a frying pan. At this temperature a piece of stale bread should brown in 50 seconds.

4 Discard the orange and lemon zest from the rice mixture. With a metal spoon, pick up some of the rice mixture—a dollop about the size of a large walnut—and with the help of a second spoon, slide it into the oil. Fry the fritters in batches until they are golden on both sides. Retrieve them with a slotted spatula and place on paper towels to drain.

5 Sprinkle each fritter very generously with sifted confectioner's sugar before serving. The fritters are good hot or cold.

Il vero lusso di una mensa sta nel dessert.
"The real luxury of a meal lies in the dessert."

From *Il piacere* by
GABRIELE D'ANNUNZIO

DOLCI

Italians love sweets, although they eat them only on special occasions. An everyday meal ends with fresh fruit; sweets are kept for Sundays, parties, family gatherings, religious days, and village *feste*.

Dolci developed differently in northern, central, and southern Italy. The dolci of the north are often little more than sweet breads, the *panettone milanese* being the prime example. The dolci of central Italy are richer, with lots of spices, nuts, candied peel, and honey, as in the *panforte* from Siena or the *certosino* from Bologna. It was also in this part of the country that there originated the *dolci al cucchiaio* (sweets that can be eaten with a spoon, such as the *zuppe inglesi*, or trifles) of Emilia-Romagna and Tuscany. In southern Italy the protagonists of dolci are almonds and candied fruits, a heritage from Arab cooking. And it is here that dolci reach the highest level of culinary art.

This being Italy, there are, of course, many exceptions to the rule. After all, the birthplace of *zabaglione*—the *dolce al cucchiaio* par excellence—is Piedmont in the north, while a *ciambella*—sweet ring-shaped bread made with potatoes, eggs and flour—is a traditional dolce of Puglia.

As they are eaten on feast days, dolci are even more regional than other kinds of food. Every patron saint, every feast day of the year, has its own special dolce, in every town in Italy. The region that has more special occasions, and more legends, associated with its dolci is Sicily. There are biscuits called *frutti di morte*—literally "fruits of death"—made with almond paste, which are eaten at the end of a meal on All Souls' Day. The *sfinci di San Giuseppe* are a sort of fritter eaten on St. Joseph's Day. For Easter Sunday a magnificent *agnello pasquale*—Easter lamb—is made in Sicily with a pastry, seasoned with cloves, that is shaped like a lamb.

Some of these special dolci have become so popular that they are now eaten year-round, not only in Italy but elsewhere, as is the case with *panettone* and *panforte*, both originally eaten only at Christmas. Others are still very localized and known only in the place where they are made. When I was in Sicily some years ago, I ate some superb soft biscuits called *olivette di Sant'Agata*. They were made of marzipan, sugar, rum, and vanilla, and are a speciality of Catania, made originally on the saint's day of Sant'Agata, a local martyr. I had never heard of *olivette* before, yet they are the best almond-based sweets I have ever had. Our Sicilian hostess insisted that we drive many, many miles along the highway to an old-fashioned *pasticceria* in Catania to buy "the only *olivette* worth eating." The lengths Italians will go in their search for excellence, as far as food is concerned, never cease to amaze me.

The tradition of excellence in Italian dolci goes back a long way. Writing in Naples at the beginning of the nineteenth century, the English noblewoman Lady Blessington commented, "Italian confectionery and ices are far superior to those of the French and the English, and their variety is infinite." A passage from *Il gattopardo* by Giuseppe Tomasi di Lampedusa gives a good idea of what Lady Blessington meant. He describes how, at the great ball, "the table was covered with pink parfaits, champagne parfaits, grey parfaits which parted creaking under the blade of the cake knife; a violin melody in major of candied morello cherries; acid notes of yellow pineapples; and the *trionfi della gola*—'triumphs of gluttony'—with the opaque green of their pistachio paste, and the shameless *minni di virgini*—'virgins' breasts'—dome-shaped pastry cupcakes stuffed with ricotta, chocolate pieces, and candied fruits and with a candied cherry stuck on top.

Torte e Crostate
CAKES AND TARTS

The emphasis of this section is on cakes containing fruit and nuts.

In Italy, cakes are often eaten as part of a meal. Cakes are also served midmorning or after supper, when they are traditionally accompanied by a glass of wine. Wine, after all, used to be the cheapest beverage, one that even poor people in the country could afford. They made their own wine, while tea or coffee had to be bought.

In all the cake and cookie recipes, I recommend the use of Italian 00 flour. This is a high-quality flour with very little flavor and very good rising properties. It is available from most supermarkets and delicatessens.

Torta di Polenta
POLENTA CAKE

Serves about 8

¾ cup blanched almonds
9 tbsp unsalted butter, cut
　into small lumps and
　softened
⅔ cup golden superfine sugar
⅔ cup all-purpose flour or
　Italian 00 flour
¾ cup coarsely ground
　polenta flour
2 tsp baking powder
pinch of sea salt
2 eggs plus 2 egg yolks
grated zest of 1 organic lemon
unsalted butter and dried
　breadcrumbs for the pan
confectioner's sugar, to
　decorate

In this peasant cake from the region of Veneto, polenta flour is used together with white flour to give the cake a grainier texture. Try to get coarsely ground polenta flour, which is available in some supermarkets and in Italian delicatessens. You *must*, if at all possible, grind the almonds yourself, instead of buying already ground almonds that are too powdery.

1　Heat the oven to 350°F.
2　Spread the almonds on a baking sheet and toast them in the oven for 7-10 minutes, or until they begin to turn golden. Remove the sheet from the oven, but leave the oven on.
3　Put the almonds in the bowl of a food processor and blitz until they are ground, but be careful not to reduce them to powder.
4　Beat together the butter and the superfine sugar until creamy. In a separate bowl, mix together the flours, baking powder, and salt and then add to the creamy butter mix. Lightly beat together the eggs and egg yolks and slowly add to the flour mixture, beating the whole time. Mix in the lemon zest.
5　Butter a 9-inch loaf pan and spread about 2 tbsp of dried breadcrumbs all over the buttered surface and then shake off the excess crumbs.
6　Spoon the cake mixture into the pan and bake for about 45 minutes, or until a skewer inserted into the center of the cake comes out clean. When the cake is cooked, it should have shrunk from the sides of the pan and be quite springy to the touch.
7　Loosen the cake all around the pan with a thin knife, invert the pan onto a wire rack, and let the cake cool. Just before you want to eat it, sprinkle sifted confectioner's sugar over the top.

Torta di Cioccolato con le Pere
CHOCOLATE AND PEAR CAKE

Serves 4–6

2.6 oz bittersweet chocolate (70% cocoa solids), broken into small pieces

5 tbsp unsalted butter, at room temperature

¾ cup confectioner's sugar, sifted

2 eggs, at room temperature, separated

1 egg yolk, at room temperature

2 pinches ground cinnamon

pinch of sea salt

1 cup all-purpose flour or Italian 00 flour

8 oz firm ripe pears, peeled and cut into ½-inch pieces

unsalted butter and dried breadcrumbs for the pan

confectioner's sugar, to decorate

I make this cake in a loaf pan, as it used to be made at my home in Milan for our *merenda*—afternoon tea. If you want to serve it as a dessert, I suggest making it in a 6-inch round pan and serving it with either whipped cream or a drizzle of heavy cream, whichever you prefer.

1 Heat the oven to 265°F. Put the chocolate in a heatproof bowl and melt it in the oven. Remove from the oven and keep in a warm place. Turn the oven heat up to 350°F.

2 Beat the butter until really soft. I use a handheld electric mixer. Gradually add the confectioner's sugar while beating constantly, then beat until light and pale yellow. (If you add all the sugar at once and start beating butter and sugar together, you will find the sugar flying everywhere except into the butter.) Add the 3 egg yolks, cinnamon, salt, and melted chocolate.

3 Whisk the 2 egg whites until stiff but not dry and then fold into the mixture by the spoonful, alternating with spoonfuls of flour. Fold lightly but thoroughly.

4 Gently mix the pear pieces into the mixture.

5 Butter a 9-inch loaf pan and sprinkle in the dried breadcrumbs. Shake the pan so the crumbs cover the buttered surface entirely and then turn the pan upside down and discard the excess crumbs. Spoon the cake mixture into the tin. Bake for about 50 minutes, or until the sides of the cake have shrunk from the pan and the cake is dry in the middle—test by inserting a wooden skewer.

6 Remove the pan from the oven, unmold the cake onto a wire rack, and leave to cool.

7 Sprinkle with sifted confectioner's sugar just before serving.

Torta di Noci
WALNUT CAKE

Serves 6–8

8 tbsp unsalted butter, at
  room temperature
1½ cups confectioner's sugar,
  sifted
3 large eggs, at room
  temperature, separated
1¼ cups walnut pieces
1 cup all-purpose flour or
  Italian 00 flour
½ tbsp baking powder
pinch of sea salt
grated zest of 1 organic lemon
¼ tsp lemon juice
unsalted butter and dried
  breadcrumbs for the pan
confectioner's sugar, to
  decorate

Buy your walnuts from a shop with a quick turnover so that they will not be old and rancid. Better still, buy the nuts in their shells at Christmas time and shell them yourself. Keep them in the freezer.

1   Heat the oven to 350°F.
2   Beat the butter until very soft. Gradually beat in the confectioner's sugar to make a smooth thick cream. Use a handheld electric mixer, if you have one.
3   Lightly beat the egg yolks together with a fork, then add gradually to the butter, mixing thoroughly to incorporate.
4   Put the walnuts in a food processor and pulse until very coarsely ground. The nuts should be grainy, not finely ground. Stir into the butter mixture.
5   Sift the flour, baking powder, and salt together and fold into the butter mixture with the lemon zest.
6   Whisk the egg whites with the lemon juice until stiff but not dry and fold into the mixture, using a metal spoon and lifting it high to incorporate more air.
7   Generously butter an 8-inch springform cake pan. Sprinkle with breadcrumbs, shake the pan to cover all the surface, and then shake out the excess crumbs. Spoon the cake mixture into the prepared pan.
8   Bake for about 45 minutes, or until the cake is done. Test by inserting a wooden skewer into the middle of the cake; it should come out dry. Unclip the side band and turn the cake over onto a wire rack to cool.
9   Sprinkle lavishly with sifted confectioner's sugar before serving.

Torta di Ricotta
RICOTTA CAKE

Serves 10–12

¾ cup raisins
1½ cups superfine sugar
8 tbsp unsalted butter, at
    room temperature
4 large eggs, at room
    temperature
grated zest of 1 organic lemon
6 tbsp potato flour
1 tbsp baking powder
½ tsp sea salt
2⅕ lbs fresh ricotta
unsalted butter for the pan
confectioner's sugar, to
    decorate

I do believe that some of the best recipes come from family *ricettari*—recipe collections. These are recipes for dishes that are suited to home cooking, and have been tested and improved over the years by generations of cooks, such as this one. This cake is gluten-free.

1   Soak the raisins in hot water for 15 minutes to plump them up.
2   Reserve 1 tbsp of the superfine sugar. Beat the butter with the remaining superfine sugar until pale and creamy and then add the eggs, one at a time. When all the eggs have been incorporated, mix in the lemon zest, potato flour, baking powder, and salt.
3   Heat the oven to 350°F.
4   Press the ricotta through the small-hole disc of a food mill, or through a sieve, directly onto the other ingredients. Do not use a food processor as it will not aerate the ricotta. Fold the ricotta thoroughly into the mixture. Drain the raisins, pat them dry with paper towels, and fold into the mixture.
5   Generously butter a 10-inch springform cake pan and sprinkle with the reserved superfine sugar to coat the bottom and sides.
6   Spoon the ricotta mixture into the pan and bake for 1–1¼ hours, or until the cake is done (it should shrink slightly from the sides of the pan). Let cool in the pan. Unmold the cake when cooled and place on a flat serving dish. Sprinkle with plenty of sifted confectioner's sugar just before serving.

La Torta Sbrisolona
CRUMBLY CAKE

Serves 6

¾ cup almonds
⅔ cup granulated sugar
1¼ cups all-purpose flour or
   Italian 00 flour
1 cup coarsely ground polenta
   flour
grated zest of 1 organic lemon
pinch of sea salt
2 egg yolks
8 tbsp unsalted butter, at
   room temperature
unsalted butter for the pan
confectioner's sugar, to
   decorate

*This cake keeps very well
for several days.*

The word *sbrisolona* is derived from *briciola* (stress on the first syllable), meaning "crumb," which is what this cake seems to consist of. If you want it less crumbly, you can cut it into slices with a sharp knife when it is still warm. But I find that part of its appeal is its rustic appearance, as well, of course, as its deliciousness. My husband's comment on it, as he munched, was, "This cake is not just moreish; once you start eating it, you can't stop."

It is an ideal cake to eat with tea or coffee in the afternoon, or with sweet wine at any time of day.

1 Heat the oven to 400°F.
2 Drop the almonds into a pan of boiling water and boil for 30 seconds after the water has come back to a boil. Drain and remove the skin by squeezing the almonds between your fingers. Spread them on a baking tray and toast them in the oven for 7–10 minutes, or until golden brown. Turn the heat down to 350°F.
3 Put the almonds in a food processor with 2 tbsp of the granulated sugar and process until they are reduced to a coarse powder.
4 In a bowl, mix the flours, the remaining granulated sugar, lemon zest, ground almonds, and salt. Add the egg yolks and work with your hands until the mixture is crumbly.
5 Add the butter to the mixture and work to incorporate it thoroughly, until the dough sticks together in a crumbly mass.
6 Generously butter an 8-inch shallow round cake pan and line the bottom with parchment paper. Spread the mixture evenly in the pan, pressing it down with your hands. Bake for 40–45 minutes, or until the cake is golden brown and a skewer inserted into the center comes out dry.
7 Turn out the cake onto a wire rack and peel off the parchment paper. Let cool. Before serving, sprinkle the cake with sifted confectioner's sugar.

Panforte
SPICY CAKE FROM SIENA

Serves 8–10

2 oz candied fruit

2 oz candied ginger

5 oz mixed candied orange, lemon, and citron peel

½ cup ground hazelnuts

⅔ cup whole hazelnuts

⅔ cup almonds

½ cup walnut pieces

1 tsp ground cinnamon

large pinch of freshly grated nutmeg

large pinch of ground cloves

large pinch of freshly ground white pepper

large pinch of ground ginger

large pinch of ground coriander

4 tbsp all-purpose flour or Italian 00 flour

1 tbsp cocoa powder

4 tbsp granulated sugar

4 tbsp light honey

oil and wax paper for the pan

1 tbsp confectioner's sugar

Panforte will keep for at least 2–3 months.

Panforte is one of the most ancient dolci. A reference to "a spicy and honeyed bread" brought back to Siena from the Middle East appears in Dante's *Inferno*. It is the traditional Christmas cake of Siena, but is now available year-round.

There are two kinds of panforte—a white one and a black one. The white is the older version. The black was created when cocoa arrived from the New World and became a fashionable ingredient.

My recipe contains a little cocoa and makes a softer panforte than commercial ones. I have also substituted candied ginger for candied pumpkin, which is hard to find outside of Italy. The ginger is an excellent substitute, both for its flavor and for being in keeping with the early origins of panforte, when spices, just arrived from the Orient, were used as a show of wealth.

1   Heat the oven to 350°F.

2   Coarsely chop all the candied fruit and peel and place in a bowl. This can be done in a food processor: cut the candied fruit and peel into pieces, put in the food processor bowl, and then pulse until all the fruit is in small pieces, being very careful not to reduce it to a paste.

3   Spread the ground hazelnuts and the whole hazelnuts on two baking sheets. Toast the ground hazelnuts in the oven for about 5 minutes and the whole hazelnuts for 10 minutes. Shake the trays gently from time to time. Add the ground hazelnuts to the candied fruit in the bowl.

4   Cool the whole hazelnuts slightly and then rub them, a few at a time, in a coarse towel to remove the skin. Place the nuts in a coarse sieve and shake to separate the skin from the nuts. Chop the nuts coarsely and add to the bowl.

Recipe continued overleaf

SPICY CAKE FROM SIENA

continued

5   Chop the almonds (still in their skins) and walnuts coarsely, either by hand or in the food processor (if you use this device, be very careful not to whiz too much; they must be very grainy, not powdery), and add to the bowl.

6   Put aside ½ tsp of the cinnamon. Sift the rest of the cinnamon, all the other spices, the flour, and cocoa powder directly into the bowl. Mix well.

7   Put the granulated sugar and honey into a small saucepan. Cook over low heat until the sugar has completely dissolved. Add to the bowl and mix very well with your hands.

8   Line the bottom of a 7-inch tart pan with a removable bottom with wax paper and grease the sides of the pan with oil. Press the mixture evenly into the pan. Let stand at room temperature for 5 hours (or longer if possible).

9   Heat the oven to 340°F.

10   Put the remaining cinnamon and the confectioner's sugar in a sieve and sprinkle over the top of the cake. Bake for about 50 minutes.

11   Remove from the oven and let cool for 10 minutes, then remove the panforte from the pan and cool completely on a wire rack. When cool, wrap in foil and store.

Pastiera Napoletana
NEAPOLITAN TART

Serves 8–10

9 oz dried wheat berries, to
    be soaked, or 14 oz canned
    cooked wheat berries
2½ cups whole milk
pinch of sea salt
grated zest of ½ organic lemon
    and ½ organic orange
2-inch piece of vanilla bean, or
    a few drops of vanilla extract
½ tsp ground cinnamon
10½ oz fresh ricotta
4 eggs, at room temperature,
    separated
2 egg yolks
1 cup superfine sugar
2 tbsp orange flower water
4 oz candied peel, cut into
    tiny pieces
unsalted butter for the pan
confectioner's sugar, to
    decorate

For the pastry
2⅓ cups all-purpose flour or
    Italian 00 flour
6 tbsp confectioner's sugar
pinch of sea salt
grated zest of ½ organic lemon
11 tbsp unsalted butter, cut
    into small pieces
3 large egg yolks

At Easter time, bakers and *pasticceri* in Naples compete with each other to produce the best *pastiere*, the beloved tart of the Neapolitans, made with wheat berries and ricotta. You can sometimes find canned wheat berries in good delicatessens and save the long labor of soaking and cooking the grain.

1 If you are using dried wheat berries, soak the grains in cold water for 48 hours. Rinse and drain them.

2 Put the soaked wheat berries in a saucepan with the milk, salt, lemon and orange zest, the vanilla bean, and cinnamon and bring to a boil. If you are using canned wheat berries, just add the lemon and orange zest, vanilla extract, and cinnamon. Simmer over the lowest possible heat for 3–4 hours or until the grain is cooked and tender. Let cool for at least 8 hours (24 hours is better) to allow the grain to swell. Remove and discard the vanilla bean.

3 Make the pastry dough: sift the flour, sugar, and salt onto a work surface. Mix in the lemon zest, then rub in the butter. Add the egg yolks and knead together briefly to make a smooth and compact dough. (The dough can also be made in a food processor.) Wrap and chill for at least 2 hours.

4 To make the filling, beat the ricotta with the 6 egg yolks. Add the superfine sugar, orange flower water, candied peel, and grain mixture. Mix very thoroughly.

5 Whisk the 4 egg whites until stiff but not dry. Fold into the grain and ricotta mixture lightly but thoroughly.

6 Heat the oven to 350°F. Butter a 10-inch springform cake pan. Roll out about two-thirds of the pastry dough and press into the tin, making sure it is of the same thickness all over the bottom and up the sides. Spoon in the filling.

7 Roll out the remaining dough and cut into long strips. Place the strips over the filling to form a lattice top. Bake for 45–50 minutes, or until the filling is set and the pastry is golden brown. Let cool and then remove from the pan. Dust with sifted confectioner's sugar before serving.

Biscotti e Frittelle
COOKIES AND FRITTERS

If you open a regional Italian cookbook, you will find more recipes for cookies than for any other type of sweet. This is because, in Italy, sweets tend to be eaten at any time of day, whereas to have a dessert at the end of a meal is unusual. Cookies are often eaten casually, as a snack, with a glass of wine, sitting around the kitchen table.

From the vast range of sweet fritters in Italy I have picked two recipes which I particularly like. Fritters are among the most ancient of foods; in Roman times they were prepared and eaten in the streets on pagan feast days, just as they are today at village feasts. Frying, after all, is the most immediate of cooking methods, and requires only a saucepan full of oil.

Baci di Dama
LADY'S KISSES

Makes about 35 cookies

1 stick unsalted butter, at
　room temperature
1 cup ground almonds
⅔ cup superfine sugar
1 tsp pure vanilla extract
pinch of sea salt
1 cup Italian 00 flour
unsalted butter for the trays
3 oz bittersweet chocolate
　(50% cocoa solids)

The name of these cookies is just as lovely as the
cookies themselves. They are a speciality of Tortona,
a town in southern Piedmont.

1　Heat the oven to 350°F.
2　Cut the butter into small pieces and place into the bowl of a food
processor together with the ground almonds. Whizz until creamy, then
add half of the sugar, the vanilla, and the salt, and blitz again until creamy.
With the machine running, spoon the flour into the bowl through the
funnel. When a soft ball forms, scoop it out and knead for 1–2 minutes.
Add 1–2 tbsp of the sugar (this absorbs the oil from the nuts) and process
to a fine powder. Add the remaining sugar, vanilla, and salt and process
again until the mixture is smooth. Transfer to a bowl.
3　With floured hands, break off pieces of the dough, the size of
cherries, and roll them into balls between the palms of your hands. Place
them on buttered baking sheets, spacing them 1 inch apart. Bake for
about 15 minutes or until golden brown. Let cool on the sheets for about
5 minutes and then transfer to a wire rack to cool completely.
4　Melt the chocolate in a bain-marie or in a heat-safe bowl in a
microwave oven. When the cookies are cool, spread a little of the
chocolate over one cookie and make a sandwich by sticking another
cookie to the chocolate.

Le Bisse
S-SHAPED COOKIES

Makes about 40 cookies

3 large eggs
1 cup superfine sugar
⅔ cup vegetable or olive oil
grated zest of 1 organic lemon
4 cups all-purpose flour or
    Italian 00 flour
pinch of sea salt
oil for baking sheets

A *bissa* is a water snake in Venetian dialect, which explains the name of these little cookies. They are to be found in any bakery or *pasticceria* in Venice, but they can easily be made at home. Use an unflavored oil.

1   In a large bowl, whisk the eggs with the sugar until pale and frothy. Add the oil and lemon zest, then fold in the flour and salt. Knead well. Wrap the dough and chill it for about 1 hour.
2   Heat the oven to 425°F.
3   Grease 2 large baking sheets with a little oil.
4   To shape each biscuit, take a small ball of dough and roll it into a sausage shape a little less than ½-inch thick and 5 inches long. Curve into the shape of an *S* and place on a baking sheet.
5   Bake for 5 minutes, then reduce the heat to 350°F and bake for another 10–15 minutes, or until pale golden. Cool slightly on the baking sheets before transferring to a wire rack to cool completely.

I Biscotti della Nonna Caterina
MY GRANDMOTHER'S COOKIES

Makes about 24 cookies

2 large egg yolks
2 tbsp rum
⅔ cup superfine sugar
1¼ cups all-purpose flour or
  Italian 00 flour
pinch of sea salt
7 tbsp unsalted butter, very
  soft but not melted
butter and flour for the
  baking sheets

There is an infinite number of "Torte della Nonna," but unfortunately none I can claim for *my* grandmother. However, she made these lovely cookies that are ideal for serving with ice cream or mousse, or to enjoy with coffee.

1 Heat the oven to 350°F.
2 Beat the egg yolks with the rum. Add the sugar and beat hard until pale.
3 Sift the flour with the salt and add gradually to the egg and sugar mixture, stirring hard the whole time.
4 Add the butter and beat until the mixture is well blended.
5 Butter and flour two baking sheets. To form the cookies, dampen your hands, pick up a little dollop of the dough, and shape it into a round. Place the balls on the sheets, leaving 2 inches between each one, as the mixture spreads out a lot while cooking. Bake for 15–20 minutes, or until deep gold.
6 Remove the sheets from the oven and transfer the cookies to a wire rack to cool. These will keep well for a week in an airtight container.

Crostoli Trentini
FRITTERS FROM NORTHERN ITALY

Serves 6

1¼ cups all-purpose flour,
  preferably Italian 00
1½ tbsp superfine sugar
½ tsp baking powder
pinch of sea salt
2 tbsp unsalted butter, at
  room temperature
1 large egg yolk
3 tbsp grappa or white rum
1–2 tbsp 2% milk
oil for frying
confectioner's sugar, to
  decorate

At Carnival time, every bakery, or *pasticceria,* in northern and central Italy makes a show of huge trays piled high with puffy golden fritters sprinkled with confectioner's sugar. They are the traditional Carnival fare, made in different shapes in various regions. Thus, there are *cenci* (rags) in Tuscany, *chiacchiere* (chatterings) in Lombardy, *galani* (ribbons) in Venice, and *sfrappole* (angel's wings) in Emilia. The dough varies only a little. What changes is the shape. The original crostoli from Trentino and Friuli are strips of dough tied together in a loose knot, but they are often shaped as I have done here, which is far easier. If you serve them at the end of a meal, hand around a bowl of whipped cream for dipping the crostoli in.

1   Set aside 2 tbsp of flour. Put the rest of the flour on a work surface. Mix in the superfine sugar, baking powder, and salt. Make a well and put in the butter, egg yolk, grappa, and milk. Mix everything together, kneading until the dough is well blended. If it is too stiff, add a little more milk; if too soft, add some of the reserved flour. (You can also make the dough in a food processor.) Knead the dough for at least 5 minutes as you would with bread or pasta dough. It should become smooth and elastic. Make a ball, wrap in plastic, and leave at room temperature for at least 1 hour.
2   Roll out the dough *very* thinly, using either a rolling pin or, better, a hand-cranked pasta machine. If you are using the machine, roll through the last notch. The thinness of the dough is the secret of good crostoli.
3   Using a pastry wheel, cut the strips of dough into lasagne-size rectangles. Make three parallel slashes in the middle of each rectangle.
4   Heat enough frying oil to come two-thirds of the way up the sides of a frying pan or a wok. When the oil is very hot (a piece of stale bread should brown in 50 seconds), fry the dough shapes in batches until pale gold and puffy. Lift the crostoli out of the oil and drain on paper towels.
5   Before serving, pile the crostoli on a dish, sprinkling every layer with sifted confectioner's sugar. They are excellent hot or at room temperature.

Frittelle di Semolino
SEMOLINA FRITTERS

Makes about 24 fritters

4 cups whole milk
½ cup granulated sugar
pared strip of organic lemon
    zest
8 tbsp unsalted butter
pinch of sea salt
1½ cups semolina
3 large egg yolks
oil for frying
2 eggs
2 cups dried breadcrumbs
confectioner's sugar, to
    decorate

These are also Carnival fritters from northern Italy. In my home they were always served with apple fritters and, of course, crostoli (see recipe on page 230).

1 Bring the milk slowly to a simmer with the granulated sugar, lemon zest, butter, and salt, stirring frequently to dissolve the sugar.

2 Add the semolina in a slow stream while beating hard with a wooden spoon to prevent lumps from forming. Continue stirring and cooking over low heat for 10 minutes. The mixture will be quite stiff. Remove from the heat to cool for 15 minutes or so. Remove and discard the lemon zest.

3 Mix in the egg yolks, one at a time, beating well to incorporate after each addition.

4 Spread the semolina mixture on a board or flat dish to a thickness of about 1 inch. Smooth it evenly with a damp spatula and let cool completely. You can leave it overnight.

5 Cut the semolina into 1-inch-wide strips and then cut the strips across to make lozenges.

6 Heat oil in a wok or in a deep frying pan to about 350°F—hot enough for a cube of stale bread to brown in 50 seconds.

7 Meanwhile, lightly beat the 2 whole eggs in a bowl and spread the breadcrumbs in a dish. Dip a piece of semolina into the egg and then coat with breadcrumbs, patting them into the semolina.

8 Fry, in two or three batches, to a lovely golden color and then put into a dish lined with paper towels to drain.

9 Serve hot or at room temperature, lavishly sprinkled with sifted confectioner's sugar.

Dolci al Cucchiaio
DESSERTS

In this section I have collected eight recipes for dolci that are served at parties—some famous, some little known, some elaborate and rich, others simple and modest, but all good and typically Italian.

Tiramisù
MASCARPONE PUDDING

Serves 6

⅔ cup strong espresso coffee
3 tbsp brandy
4 tbsp superfine sugar
2 oz bittersweet chocolate
  (70% cocoa solids)
2 large eggs, at room
  temperature, separated
1 large egg yolk
9 oz mascarpone
about 20 Savoiardi cookies

For the decoration
coffee beans
candied violets (optional)

*Savoiardi are available from
Italian delicatessens and
good supermarkets. If you
cannot find them, make your
own sponge finger cookies—
ordinary sponge fingers or
boudoir cookies will not be
absorbent enough.*

A book on dolci would hardly be complete without including the most popular of them all, tiramisù. Surprisingly, considering its popularity, tiramisù is a relatively new arrival even on the Italian scene. In the 1970s it was only known in the region where it originated, Veneto.

1 Mix together the hot coffee and brandy. Add ½ tbsp of the superfine sugar and mix until the sugar has dissolved. Set aside to cool.
2 Grate about one-quarter of the chocolate and cut the rest into small pieces.
3 Beat the 3 egg yolks with the sugar until very pale and softly peaked. Fold the mascarpone in gradually and mix very thoroughly until the mixture is smooth and without any lumps.
4 Whisk the 2 egg whites until stiff but not dry and fold gradually into the mascarpone and egg yolk mixture.
5 In a small bowl set aside about 2 tbsp of the mascarpone mixture, then cover the bowl and put in the fridge to chill.
6 Take a 1-quart oven dish (oval, round, or square—whichever you prefer). Dip a third of the cookies, one at a time, into the coffee and brandy mixture, turning them over once or twice until they become pale brown and soggy. Lay them, one by one, over the bottom of the dish. Spread 2–3 tbsp of the mascarpone cream over them and sprinkle with about half the chocolate pieces. Dip more cookies in the coffee mixture and make another layer. Cover with about half of the remaining mascarpone cream and sprinkle the remaining chocolate pieces over the top. Cover with a final layer of soaked cookies. Pour any remaining coffee mixture over the cookies and top with the remaining cream.
7 Cover the pudding tightly and put it in the fridge to chill for about 6 hours.
8 Serve the pudding straight from the fridge, spreading the reserved mascarpone cream over the top of the pudding and sprinkling with the grated chocolate.

Le Dita degli Apostoli
PANCAKES STUFFED WITH RICOTTA

Serves 8–10

For the pancakes
5 large eggs
2 tbsp superfine sugar
1 cup all-purpose flour
pinch of sea salt
1 cup 2% milk
butter for frying the pancakes

For the stuffing
1⅓ lbs fresh ricotta
3 tbsp heavy cream
1¼ cups superfine sugar
grated zest of 1 organic lemon
grated zest of 1 organic
    orange
grated zest of 1 organic
    clementine
1½ tbsp finely chopped
    candied peel
2 oz bittersweet chocolate
    (70% cocoa solids), chopped
    into small pieces
2 tbsp dark rum
confectioner's sugar, to
    decorate

The odd name of this recipe from Puglia, the heel of the Italian boot, means "apostles' fingers." I can only suppose the pancakes were given this name because their appearance calls to mind long fingers, raised to give a blessing.

This is the recipe developed by my colleague and dear friend Alice Wooledge Salmon from the original recipe by the cooking instructor Paola Pettini, who showed us how to make this dish when we went to Puglia for a gastronomic tour.

1 To make the pancakes, beat the eggs with the sugar. Mix in the flour and salt and then gradually add the milk while beating constantly. The batter should be fairly liquid. Let rest for 1 hour.
2 Meanwhile, prepare the stuffing. Press the ricotta through a sieve into a bowl and fold in the cream and superfine sugar. Add all the other ingredients (except the confectioner's sugar) and mix very thoroughly. Chill.
3 Make very thin pancakes in an 11-inch pan. (If not using a nonstick pan, grease it lightly with melted butter.) You should get twelve large pancakes.
4 Lay the pancakes on the work surface and spread the stuffing thinly all over each one. Roll them up tightly.
5 Cut each "finger" into three or four pieces, place on a dish, and sprinkle with sifted confectioner's sugar. These are traditionally served at room temperature.

Crema Mascarpone
MASCARPONE AND RUM CREAM

Serves 4

2 large eggs, separated
2 tbsp superfine sugar
2 tbsp dark rum
8 oz mascarpone
1 tsp lemon juice
12 amaretti cookies

Similar to the ubiquitous tiramisù, this dessert is lighter and more subtle. In my family it used to be called "la crema del principe," and it is indeed a royal dessert, smooth and delicate.

The cream can be prepared ahead of time up to step 3. Add the egg whites no longer than 1 hour before serving. Serve with amaretti cookies, whose dark, almondy flavor is ideal with this dessert.

1 Whisk the egg yolks with the sugar until light and mousselike, then beat in the rum.
2 Press the mascarpone through a fine sieve and fold into the egg yolk mixture.
3 Whisk the egg whites with the lemon juice until stiff but not dry and fold gently into the mixture until the cream is smooth. Spoon the mixture into long stem glasses and place 1 amaretto cookie on the top. Pass the rest of the amaretti around on a dish. Keep the cream chilled until ready to serve.

La Meringa Farcita
MERINGUE FILLED WITH MARRONS GLACÉS, CHOCOLATE, AND CREAM

Serves 6–8

For the meringue

4 large egg whites, at room temperature

1 tsp lemon juice

1 cup superfine sugar

For the filling

2 large egg whites

3 tbsp superfine sugar

2 cups whipping cream

4 tbsp dark rum

8 oz marrons glacés, chopped into small pieces

3½ oz bittersweet chocolate (70% cocoa solids), chopped into small pieces

2 tbsp pistachio nuts, blanched, peeled, and chopped

The meringue in this recipe is Italian meringue, which is less fragile than Swiss meringue made with uncooked egg whites. However, if you find it easier, you can make the more common Swiss meringue, as you would for a pavlova.

1   Heat the oven to 300°F.

2   Make an Italian meringue as follows. Whisk the egg whites with the lemon juice until stiff. Put the bowl over a saucepan of simmering water and continue whisking while gradually adding the sugar. Whisk until the mixture is warm, silky looking, and forming soft peaks.

3   Draw two 8-inch circles on parchment paper as a guide for the meringue shapes. Place the paper guides on one or two baking sheets. Spoon the meringue over both circles, smoothing it out to the edges of the circles with an offset spatula. Bake for about 45 minutes, or until the meringue is set. Remove the meringue discs from the paper and let cool.

4   For the filling, whisk the egg whites in a bowl until stiff. Place the bowl over a saucepan of simmering water and gradually add the sugar, while whisking constantly. When the mixture is warm, remove from the heat and place the base of the bowl in a basin of cold water to cool. This stiff egg white mixture makes the filling lighter.

5   Whip the cream. Fold in the egg white mixture.

6   Add the rum, marrons glacés, chocolate, and pistachios and mix well until everything is evenly distributed.

7   Place one of the meringue discs on a flat dish. Spread two-thirds of the filling over it and put the other disc on top. Cover with the remaining filling. Chill for at least 6 hours before serving.

Mele alle Mandorle e al Vino Bianco

SAUTÉED APPLES WITH ALMONDS AND WHITE WINE

Serves 6

6 large apples of equal size, such as Granny Smith or other tart dessert apples
1 organic lemon
4 tbsp unsalted butter
3 cloves
⅔ cup Calvados
⅓ cup superfine sugar, or more according to the sweetness of the apples
½ cup sweet white wine
½ tsp ground cinnamon
¾ cup sliced almonds
1¼ cups heavy cream
4 tbsp confectioner's sugar, sifted

A lovely dessert, this dish combines the light, fresh flavor of fruit with the richness of a brandy-laced cream.

1   Peel the apples, cut them in half, and remove the cores. Make four incisions in the round side of each half, taking care not to cut right through it.

2   Remove the zest from half the lemon using a peeler, taking care to leave behind the bitter white pith. Squeeze the juice from the whole lemon and set aside.

3   Heat the butter in a very large sauté pan in which the apple halves will fit comfortably. Add the lemon zest and cloves to the butter and when the butter foam begins to subside, slide in the apples, cut side down. Sauté until golden, then turn the halves over and brown the round side. This will take about 8 minutes. Shake the pan occasionally to prevent the apples from sticking.

4   Turn the heat up, add one-third of the Calvados, and let it bubble away for 30 seconds. Turn the heat down to low and add the superfine sugar, wine, lemon juice, and ⅔ cup of hot water. Cover the pan with the lid or a piece of foil and cook for 5 minutes. Turn the apples over carefully and continue cooking until they are tender. Cooking time varies according to the quality of the apples; do not overcook them or they may break. If necessary add a couple of spoonfuls of hot water during the cooking.

5   When the apples are ready—test them by piercing them with the blade of a small knife through their thickest part—transfer them gently to a dish using a slotted spoon. Let cool.

6   Remove the lemon zest and cloves from the pan. Add the cinnamon and almonds and sauté over a moderate heat for 5 minutes, stirring constantly, until the syrup is thick and the almonds are caramelized. Remove from the heat.

7   Whip the cream. Add the remaining Calvados and the confectioner's sugar and whip again. Spread the cream over a shallow serving dish. Make twelve hollows in the cream with the back of a spoon and lay the apple halves in the hollows, cut side up. Spoon the syrup-coated almonds over the apples. Serve at room temperature.

Frutta Cotta al Forno
STEWED MIXED FRUIT

Serves 4

2 pears, Comice or Bartlett

2 apples, Granny Smith or
    Cox's

2 bananas

2 organic oranges

6 pitted prunes

grated zest of 1 small organic
    lemon

3 tbsp light brown sugar

⅔ cup robust red wine, such
    as barbera

heavy cream for serving

The simplicity of this dish should not deter you from trying it. The fruit, well-cooked yet still in neat pieces, absorbs the flavor of the wine and its deep color. Buy plump, moist prunes that don't need to be soaked.

1 Heat the oven to 350°F.

2 Peel and core the pears and apples. Peel the bananas and oranges. Slice them all quite thinly, keeping them separate.

3 Lay the sliced fruit in layers in a 1-quart gratin dish, arranging the slices so that each fruit is topped with a different fruit. Scatter the prunes here and there and sprinkle with the lemon zest and sugar. Pour the wine over the fruit and cover the dish. Bake for 30 minutes.

4 Uncover the dish and press the fruit down with a slotted spoon to release more liquid. Bake for another 15 minutes. Serve warm with the cream.

Zuppa Inglese
CAKE AND CUSTARD PUDDING

Serves 6

⅔ cup heavy cream
12 oz best pound cake, cut
   into ¼-inch slices
4 tbsp rum
4 tbsp cherry brandy
2 egg whites, at room
   temperature
5 tbsp confectioner's sugar,
   sifted
1 tbsp superfine sugar

For the custard
2 cups whole milk
2 strips of organic lemon zest
3 large egg yolks
⅓ cup superfine sugar
6 tbsp all-purpose flour or
   Italian 00 flour

Zuppa Inglese used to appear on almost every menu in restaurants within Italy and elsewhere, just as tiramisù does today. And, like tiramisù, it can be delicious or disastrous. It all depends on the balance of the ingredients used.

The name Zuppa Inglese—"English soup"—is a mystery. Like other Italian writers on the subject, I think the dish must owe its origin to the English trifle, which would have been brought to Tuscany and Naples by the English in the eighteenth and nineteenth centuries. The liqueur Alchermes, used in Italy, is hardly available elsewhere. Cherry brandy is a good substitute.

1 First make the custard. Bring the milk to a boil with the lemon zest and set aside.
2 Beat the egg yolks with the sugar until pale yellow and light. Beat the flour into the mixture and then slowly pour in the hot milk.
3 Transfer the custard to a heavy-bottomed saucepan and place over very low heat. Cook, stirring the whole time, until the custard is very thick and an occasional bubble breaks through the surface. Simmer very gently for a couple of minutes longer. Place the base of the saucepan in a bowl of iced water to cool the custard quickly. Stir frequently.
4 Whip the cream until soft peaks form. When the custard is cold, fold in the cream.
5 Line a 2-quart soufflé dish with plastic wrap, which will help in unmolding the pudding.
6 Line the bottom of the soufflé dish with slices of cake, plugging any holes with pieces of cake. Sprinkle with some rum and spread a couple of spoonfuls of custard over the cake.
7 Cover with another layer of cake, moisten it with cherry brandy, and then spread some custard over the cake. Repeat these layers, ending with the cake moistened with either the rum or the brandy.

8   Cover the pudding with plastic wrap and refrigerate for at least 8 hours or, better still, 24 hours, to allow all the flavors to combine.

9   Some 6 hours before you want to serve the pudding, heat the oven to 230°F. Whisk the egg whites with the confectioner's sugar until stiff. Remove the pudding from the fridge and turn it out onto a round serving dish that can be put in the oven at a low temperature. Peel off the plastic wrap, spread the meringue all over the pudding, and sprinkle with the superfine sugar. Bake until the meringue is dry and very pale blond in color, 20–25 minutes. Let cool and then place the pudding back in the fridge to chill for at least 2 hours before serving.

Zuccotto
FLORENTINE CREAM PUDDING

Serves 8–10

½ cup blanched almonds

½ cup hazelnuts

3 tbsp brandy

3 tbsp amaretto

3 tbsp maraschino or other
sweet liqueur

9 oz pound cake, cut into
¼-inch-thick slices

5 oz bittersweet chocolate
(70% cocoa solids)

2 cups whipping cream

¾ cup confectioner's sugar,
sifted

For the decoration

2 tbsp confectioner's sugar,
sifted

1 tbsp cocoa powder, sifted

This is a rich, creamy pudding from Florence. Its domed shape is like half a pumpkin (*zucca* in Italian) and it is decorated with alternating brown and white segments, like the cupola of Florence Cathedral. This is the classic shape of the zuccutto, but I am afraid I do not make it like that. As you can see from the photograph, I use an oval fluted mold with a 1.5-quart capacity, which I love, and I do not bother with all the fidgeting of the white and brown segments to resemble the cupola of Florence's main *duomo*. Instead, I just shower the top with sifted confectioner's sugar and cocoa powder. If you want, you can use a glass mixing bowl of the same capacity and your zuccotto will be just as good.

1   Heat the oven to 400°F. Put the almonds and hazelnuts on separate baking trays and toast in the oven for 5 minutes. Then, with a rough towel, rub off as much of the hazelnut skins as you can. Roughly chop the almonds and hazelnuts and set aside.

2   Mix the three liqueurs together. Line the inside of a 1.5-quart dome-shaped mold or glass bowl with plastic wrap and then with cake slices, reserving some for the top. Moisten the cake with most of the liqueur mixture.

3   Melt 2 oz of the chocolate in a small bowl set over a pan of simmering water (or in a microwave); set aside. Cut the remaining chocolate into small pieces.

4   Whip the cream with the confectioner's sugar until stiff. Fold in the almonds, hazelnuts, and chocolate pieces.

5   Divide the cream mixture in half and spoon one portion into the mold, spreading it evenly all over the cake lining the bottom and sides. Fold the melted chocolate into the remaining cream mixture and spoon it into the mold to fill the cavity. Cover the pudding with the reserved cake and moisten it with the rest of the liqueur. Cover the mold with plastic wrap and refrigerate for at least 12 hours.

FLORENTINE CREAM PUDDING

continued

6   To unmold, place a piece of wax or parchment paper and then a piece of cardboard over the top of the mold. Turn the whole thing over so that the pudding falls out. Remove the mold and peel off the plastic wrap.

7   Now, if you want to make the classic zuccotto, cut out a 15-inch circle of wax or parchment paper. Fold it in two to make a half-moon, then fold this in two to make a triangle. Fold the triangle in two again to make a thinner triangle. Open up and cut out each alternate section, without cutting the paper through at the top.

8   Dust the whole dome with some sifted confectioner's sugar. Mix the 2 tbsp of sifted confectioner's sugar with the cocoa powder. Place the cut-out circle of paper over the dome and sprinkle the cocoa and sugar mixture over the cut-out sections. Remove the paper carefully without spoiling the pattern. Transfer the pudding to a flat round serving dish, using the cardboard for support. Serve chilled.

Gelati e Sorbetti
ICE CREAMS AND SORBETS

I could write a whole book on these sweets, so choosing just a few recipes was quite difficult. Gelati and sorbetti had their origins in Italy, and it was the Italian emigrants who took them to the US, where people have now adopted them and made them their own.

I find that only in Italy can you still find excellent ices in specialist *gelaterie*—ice cream shops where the ice creams are made on the premises. The choice is bewildering. Some new favorite flavors, such as tiramisù and zuppa inglese, compete with the lovely old classics, gelato al caffè or al limone. The fruit water ices are the best because of the strong flavor of the fruit, ripened in the hot sun.

Spumone al Cioccolato
FROZEN CHOCOLATE CREAM LOAF

Serves 8

5 oz bittersweet chocolate
  (70% cocoa solids)
1½ cups whole milk
4 large egg yolks
⅔ cup superfine sugar
4 level tsp all-purpose flour
  or Italian 00 flour
4 tbsp strong espresso coffee
1¼ cups whipping cream,
  very cold
12 amaretti cookies (optional)
½ cup Marsala or medium
  sherry (optional)

A spumone is a kind of soft ice cream. Spumoni are always molded in a pan, usually a loaf pan, and served cut into slices like a pâté. This is the recipe for a chocolate spumone with a delicate creamy flavor. You need to use best-quality chocolate with a high cocoa content. This spumone is particularly delicious covered with amaretti that have been lightly soaked in either Marsala or sherry.

1   Melt the chocolate in a bain-marie or slowly in a microwave-safe bowl in the microwave, checking every 15 seconds.

2   Heat the milk to simmering point.

3   Meanwhile, beat the egg yolks with the sugar until pale and light. Add the flour and beat well. Slowly pour in the hot milk, beating constantly. Transfer the custard to a heavy-bottomed saucepan and cook over the lowest heat, stirring constantly, until the custard thickens and some bubbles break on the surface. Cook for a couple of minutes longer, stirring constantly.

4   Mix the melted chocolate and the coffee into the custard. Put the base of the saucepan in a basin of cold water to cool the custard quickly. Stir every now and then.

5   Whip the cream. When the custard has cooled, fold in the cream.

6   Line a 9-inch loaf pan with foil or plastic wrap. Spoon the mixture into the pan and freeze overnight.

7   Remove from the freezer 1 hour before serving. Unmold onto a rectangular dish and cut into slices to serve.

Note: If you wish to cover this dessert with amaretti cookies, crush the cookies in a bowl, then sprinkle them with Marsala or sherry, and stir through. Lay them over the spumone just before serving.

Semifreddo di Zabaglione al Caffè
FROZEN COFFEE ZABAGLIONE

Serves 6

3 large eggs, separated
2 large egg yolks
⅔ cup superfine sugar
⅔ cup Marsala or medium
    sweet sherry
pinch of ground cinnamon
4 tbsp strong espresso coffee
1 cup whipping cream
¾ cup confectioner's sugar,
    sifted
coffee beans and whipped
    cream, to decorate

A "semifreddo" cannot freeze hard because of the high sugar content in the meringue. This is why it is called "half-cold" and why its consistency is so soft and voluptuous.

1   To make zabaglione, I use a stainless steel round-bottomed bowl, which I place over a pan of water. Whatever bowl you use, the bottom of the bowl must not touch the water. Put all 5 egg yolks into the bowl, add the superfine sugar, and whisk vigorously until pale. Add the Marsala or sherry and the cinnamon. Turn on the heat, bring the water to a simmer, and continue beating for a minute or so. The mixture will soon become soft and foamy like whipped cream. Remove from the heat and add the coffee. Place in a sink full of cold water to cool. Stir the zabaglione every now and then to prevent a skin from forming.
2   Whip the cream and fold into the zabaglione lightly but thoroughly.
3   Whisk the egg whites until firm. Gradually add the confectioner's sugar and continue beating until the meringue forms stiff peaks. Fold it 1 or 2 spoonfuls at a time into the egg yolk mixture.
4   Spoon the zabaglione mixture into a glass bowl or individual glasses and freeze overnight.
5   Decorate with coffee beans and dollops of whipped cream before serving.

Sorbetto al Mandarino
CLEMENTINE SORBET

Serves 4

2 cups superfine sugar
pared zest of 1 organic lemon
pared zest of 1 organic orange
1¼ cups freshly squeezed
   clementine juice
4 tbsp freshly squeezed
   orange juice
4 tbsp freshly squeezed lemon
   juice
2 tbsp white rum

A sorbet is not a winter dessert, so it might seem strange to have a recipe for clementine sorbet when clementines are at their very best in December. But a sorbet at Christmas is often a welcome dessert, as it refreshes and cleanses a palate that's slightly jaded from the onslaught of rich food. You will need an ice cream machine to make this dish.

1   Put the sugar, lemon and orange zest, and 1¼ cups of water in a heavy-bottomed saucepan. Bring slowly to a boil and simmer for 5 minutes. Allow to cool, then strain the syrup.
2   Strain the fruit juices and add to the cold syrup with the rum. Mix well and pour the mixture into an ice cream machine. Freeze according to the manufacturer's instructions.

Cassata Gelata
ICED CASSATA

Serves 6–8

2½ cups whole milk
grated zest of 1 organic lemon
5 large egg yolks
¾ cup superfine sugar
¼ cup blanched almonds
¼ cup shelled pistachios
⅔ cup whipping cream
1 oz candied fruit, chopped
1 tbsp confectioner's sugar,
    sifted

This is the original, homemade, recipe for the cassata that is now sold frozen in supermarkets. It is quite a lengthy dish to make, but it is easy even if you do not have an ice cream machine. You can substitute bits of good-quality chocolate for the pistachios.

1   In a saucepan heat the milk with the lemon zest until just hot.

2   Put the egg yolks in a heavy-bottomed saucepan, add the superfine sugar, and beat with a handheld electric mixer until pale. Gradually pour in the hot milk and place the saucepan over very low heat. Slowly cook the custard while beating with a wooden spoon until it begins to thicken. At this point, quickly remove the pan from the heat and place it in a sink of cold water. Leave it there to get cold, while giving the custard a good stir every now and then. When it is cold, either pour it into an ice cream machine and follow the manufacturer's instructions or, if you do not have an ice cream machine, place it as is in the freezer. Leave it until just frozen, but not too hard.

3   Place a 5-cup bombe mold (or a metal mold and a piece of foil to act as a lid) in the freezer to chill for 30 minutes.

4   Spoon the custard ice cream into the chilled mold, lining the bottom and sides evenly but leaving a hole in the middle. Return the mold to the freezer.

5   Put the almonds and the pistachio nuts in a frying pan and toast them until golden. Shake the pan very often. Transfer the nuts to a board and chop them coarsely, or do this in a food processor, being very careful not to blitz them too much and reduce them to powder. You want the nuts to be the size of grains of rice.

6   Whip the cream and fold in the nuts, candied fruit and confectioner's sugar. Spoon this mixture into the center of the ice cream–lined mold and return it to the freezer. Freeze for at least 4 hours.

7   About an hour before serving, remove the lid from the mold, cover the mold with a flat dish, and turn the whole thing over. Put the mold, on the dish, in the fridge. By the time you wish to serve the cassata, you should be able to lift the mold off easily. If the cassata is still frozen onto the mold, dip the mold quickly into very hot water for a few seconds.

Gelatine di Frutta
FRUIT GELATINS

The image of fruit gelatins has been debased by the synthetic-tasting gelatins made from packets of flavored powder dissolved in water. In Italy these do not exist; the Italians have always made their gelatins from the juice of fresh fruit. These gelatins were particularly popular in the Renaissance, when they were made in various shapes and guises to become the centerpieces of lavishly adorned tables.

Here are two fruit gelatins, one for the summer and one for the winter. I use leaf gelatin, not gelatin powder, as the latter has an unpleasant gluey flavor and dissolves less evenly. Leaf gelatin can be found at specialty food shops.

Gelatina di Arancia
ORANGE GELATIN

Serves 4–6

3 tsp leaf gelatine
¾ cup superfine sugar
1¼ cups freshly squeezed
   orange juice, strained
4 tbsp freshly squeezed lemon
   juice, strained
2 tbsp Grand Marnier
4 tbsp white rum

Buy oranges with full flavor and the right amount of acidity. I prefer Italian or Spanish oranges, which have these highly important attributes.

1   Soak the gelatine leaves in cold water for 5–6 minutes, until soft.

2   Put the sugar and the strained fruit juices in a saucepan. Bring very slowly to a boil and simmer until the sugar has dissolved, stirring occasionally. Remove from the heat.

3   Put ¾ cup of water in a saucepan. Lift the gelatine leaves out of the soaking water and squeeze out the liquid. Add to the pan of water and heat gently until the gelatine has dissolved, beating constantly with a small whisk. Pour into the fruit syrup and add the Grand Marnier and rum. Stir very thoroughly and allow to cool.

4   Grease a 3-cup gelatin mold with a mild vegetable oil or almond oil. Pour the mixture into the mold and chill for at least 6 hours or overnight.

5   To serve, immerse the mold for a few seconds in a basin of warm water. Place a flat dish over the mold and turn the whole thing upside down. Pat the mold and give a few jerks to the dish. The gelatin should now turn out easily. Put the mold back on the gelatin to cover it and replace the dish in the fridge until ready to serve.

Note: I like to serve this orange jelly with sliced oranges topped with passionfruit. For four people you will need 4–5 oranges, 2 tbsp superfine sugar, and 3 passionfruits. Peel the oranges and slice very thinly. Put them in a bowl and gently mix in the sugar. Cut the passionfruits in half and with a pointed spoon scoop out the little green seeds and the juice, spreading them all over the orange slices. Make the dish at least 2 hours in advance and keep refrigerated, covered with plastic wrap.

Gelatina di More o di Ribes
BLACKBERRY OR RED CURRANT GELATIN

Serves 4–5

3 tsp leaf gelatine
⅔ cup superfine sugar
piece of vanilla bean
1¼ cups pure blackberry or
   red currant juice
4 tbsp Marsala
juice of ½ lemon
⅔ cup whipping cream

This is a thick gelatin, rich in color and flavor, suitable for serving in individual bowls. I suggest you make your own fruit juice by boiling the fruit for 2–3 minutes and then straining it through a sieve lined with cheesecloth.

1 Soak the gelatin leaves in cold water for 5–6 minutes, until soft.
2 Put the sugar, ½ cup of water, and the vanilla bean in a small saucepan. Bring slowly to a boil, stirring frequently. Simmer for about 10 minutes. Remove from the heat.
3 Squeeze the water out of the gelatin leaves. Add the gelatin to the sugar syrup and let dissolve, whisking constantly.
4 When the gelatin is thoroughly dissolved, remove the pan from the heat. Remove and discard the vanilla bean. Add the fruit juice, Marsala, and lemon juice and mix very thoroughly.
5 Spoon the fruit syrup into four or five bowls. Chill in the fridge for at least 6 hours.
6 Whip the cream and drop a spoonful on top of each bowl. Return to the fridge until you are ready to serve the gelatin.

LIST OF RECIPES

Risotti

Dolci

INDEX

R

NOTES FOR COOKS

Butter: I use unsalted butter, which is healthier and tastes better than the salted variety. You should use unsalted butter in all sweets.

Eggs: I always use free-range and/or organic eggs.

Flour: I recommend you use Italian 00 flour, a high-quality flour that is milled very finely, with no additives. It is much easier to work with when making pasta and pastry, and when I use it in dolci recipes, I find it gives a more delicate flavor. Italian 00 flour is available in specialty Italian shops and good supermarkets.

Lemons and other citrus fruits: I buy organic or unwaxed fruit because I often use the rind.

Oil: I use plain olive oil if I am mixing it with butter for frying. Otherwise, I use extra virgin olive oil, especially for dressing salads or when I'm adding it at the end of cooking.

Parmesan: I use mostly Parmigiano-Reggiano, particularly when I want to add it grated at the end. But a good padano or even a good mature cheddar, although less flavorful, is fine for using in stuffings and white sauces.

Salt: I use only sea salt, coarse or fine, depending on what I am making and the method used.